Teachers
and
Teaching

Peter Dawson

Basil Blackwell

To Patrick and Tony, who have taught me many things.

© 1984 Peter Dawson

First published
Basil Blackwell Limited
108 Cowley Road, Oxford OX4 1JF, England

British Library Cataloguing in Publication Data

Dawson, Peter
  Teachers and teaching.
  1. Teaching
  I. Title
  371.1'02   LB1025.2

  ISBN 0-631-13174-4
  ISBN 0-631-13175-2 Pbk

Cover photograph by Frank Smith, Media Resources Officer, Eltham Green School

Typeset in 11/13pt Garamond by
Freeman Graphic, Tonbridge, Kent, England.
Printed in Great Britain

Teachers and Teaching

Contents

by the same author

Making a Comprehensive Work

Preface

This book has been written several times. Originally scheduled for completion a year ago, it has been delayed time and again by developments in the education system which have called for revision of the text. But waiting for education to reach a sufficient state of immobility for an account of it to be precisely up to date has proved a futile exercise, rather like waiting for the sea to stand still in order that one may get it exactly right in a painting.

In *The Ascent of Man,* Jacob Bronowski observes that human achievement is not a museum of finished constructions, but a progress. The good news and the bad news is that education in England and Wales is at this time further from being a finished construction than at any in its history. That is good news because so much about it is unsatisfactory; it is bad news because teachers and pupils alike could do with a period of stability. One thing is for sure: by the time this book is published, the teaching profession will no longer be in exactly the condition it describes.

Harry Taylor would approve of this preface. He was always telling me about how schools had changed since he was a boy at the beginning of the century. He was in his eighties and used to sweep the playgrounds at the London comprehensive where I was head-master for ten years. Officials would from time to time observe that he was too old for the job, but he was the most reliable person on the campus bar none, and the children loved him. He once wrote a piece of doggerel about the school while he was in hospital, delivering it to me on his return for all the world like a small boy handing over an absence note. He was, of course, very conscious of the monstrous size of our establishment:

> I pause a moment, holding broom,
> And gaze up at the floors that loom
> To six or seven stories high
> And think: 'How great. How small am I.'

Despite all the changes Harry had seen in his lifetime, he was keenly aware that some things had remained the same. He found echoes of the past in what went on around him and realised that he and the youngsters who chattered to him every morning had a good deal in common:

> And when they all get settled in,
> I listen to the hymns they sing,
> Reminding me of, now and then,
> When I left school in nineteen–ten.

> Some years have passed and still I'm here,
> Facing four seasons of the year;
> I talk to pupils, just a few,
> And still I learn at eighty-two.

The spirit of Harry Taylor is abroad in this book. For all that education had changed, and in ways of which he disapproved, he still held teachers in high esteem. 'If they aren't respected', he once said to me, 'children might as well not come to school.' Then he added: 'The trouble is, some teachers don't have enough respect for themselves these days.' Harry would have agreed with Walter Bagehot if he had heard of him. In his *Literary Studies,* that great guardian of the English way of life wrote: 'A schoolmaster should have an atmosphere of awe, and walk wonderingly, as if he was amazed at being himself.'

My thanks to Harry Taylor, an amateur educator who knew as much about teaching as some classroom professionals. My thanks also to others whose influence has brought this book to birth. I name in particular that *éminence grise* of the teaching profession, Geoffrey Barrell, whose perceptive comments on the manuscript have been made with that air of apologetic authority that distinguishes the true master in the art of human relations. The knowledge and expertise of Industrial Relations and Personnel Consultants (IRPC) have also been employed in checking my manuscript, and I owe a great debt to David Brierley of that organisation. Such errors as remain are, of course, attributable to me.

The tolerance and understanding of my colleagues at the headquarters of the Professional Association of Teachers have contributed to the successful completion of this work. The office staff of a teachers' trade union acquire a unique perspective on the teaching profession, and there is probably a book to be written about that one day. To my senior executive colleagues, Geoffrey Gospel and John Andrews, my thanks for the extent to which their thinking has shaped my own. A similar word is due to the members of the Council of the Professional Association of Teachers. That body truly reflects the variety of people who go to make up the teaching profession, containing as it does teachers in nursery, infant, junior and secondary schools; people lecturing in colleges; teachers in both the state and independent sectors of the education service; head teachers, deputy heads, departmental and pastoral heads and ordinary classroom practitioners. The accumulated wisdom and experience of such a group of men and women has obviously had a significant influence upon what appears in the following pages.

There remains one person to whom I wish to offer a special word of thanks as I finally get this book off my chest, namely my wife. Much is owed to her unflagging enthusiasm when it seemed that life was too busy to allow for such things as the writing of books. I offer her my profound gratitude for typing and retyping the manuscript, and for restoring my soul after meetings of the Burnham Committee.

In conclusion, it needs to be made clear that the analysis of the teaching profession which follows is my own. The views expressed belong entirely to me except in those places where it is made clear that they represent policies of the Professional Association of Teachers. If a certain element of dogmatism emerges here and there, that is nothing more than the natural effect upon the human personality of twenty years as a schoolmaster. If caught in an unguarded moment, I would probably have to admit to feeling the same way about educational debate as Winston Churchill did about democracy: 'It involves the occasional necessity of deferring to the opinions of other people.'

Peter Dawson
Easter 1983

One

The Teacher's Function

Everyone knows about teachers. They come second only to mothers-in-law as a subject for imitation and derision. The average British adult, having enjoyed or endured a dozen or more years of compulsory schooling, considers himself well acquainted with the sort of people who make a living in the classroom and not at all unable to distinguish the competent from the incompetent. He also knows that the condition of a school depends not upon the structure of the curriculum or the splendour of the premises but the quality of the teachers.

Great writers have gone further and taken the state of the teaching profession as a measure of the condition of the nation. Through the illiterate, bullying schoolmaster at Dotheboys Hall, Charles Dickens had almost as much to say about the exercise of power in nineteenth-century England as his contemporaries Jeremy Bentham and John Stuart Mill. Reference to the school system as a means of influencing the power structure grows apace in our own century, emphasising the significance of Adolf Hitler's observation:

> It is between the ages of ten and seventeen that youth exhibits both the greatest enthusiasm and the greatest idealism. It is for this period of their lives that we must provide them with the best possible instructors and leaders. For once youth has been won over to an idea an action like that of yeast sets in.
>
> (*Hitler's Table Talk,* translated by Cameron and
> Stevens with introduction by Hugh Trevor-Roper)

The identity of the monster responsible for those words does not detract from their truth, but rather serves to underline their implications.

The importance of teachers being widely acknowledged, the readiness of the adult population to pass judgement on them is not surprising. Thus, schools are held more or less responsible for most of the social ills which beset us from time to time. If young people fail to conduct themselves in a civilised manner, it is because of lack of discipline in the classroom. If they are unable to find employment on leaving school, it is because what they have been taught has not been sufficiently relevant to the needs of the labour market. If they challenge the law, it is because they have not been led to respect it by their teachers. If they decline to challenge it and meekly accept establishment values, it is because they have not had brought home to them the need for each new generation to question the social structure and move civilisation forward.

The latter view is nowhere better depicted than in *Teaching as a Subversive Activity* by Neil Postman and Charles Weingartner. The significance of the title is underlined by a drawing on the cover showing an apple for teacher in the form of a bomb with a fuse attached. The reader learns that the principal task of the teaching profession is to turn children into crap detectors (*sic*), and that the function of a school is to equip young people to identify and reject those values in society that appear not to serve their purposes. With a sweeping condemnation of most educational provision, the authors assert: 'There are few men currently working as professional educators who have anything germane to say about changing our educational system to fit realities.'

The dichotomy which lies at the heart of a teacher's role makes it inevitable that, whatever approach he takes to a given situation, there will be those ready to applaud and others to attack what he does. Attempting to be both an upholder of law and order and a catalyst frequently places him in an impossible situation. As both the passer-on of society's most hallowed traditions and an encourager of those who wish to argue for their overthrow, nervous breakdown shadows his footsteps.

His dilemma is well illustrated by reference to his duty to control the behaviour of children and to his choice of teaching style. The very suggestion that there is to be a staff debate about discipline or teaching methods will raise the temperature in a school before the first exchanges are uttered. Media analysis of these issues has sold more newspapers, raised the rating of more television programmes and provided the basis for more populist political speechmaking than the condition of sterling, which at once reflects the passion with which different views are held and every man's conviction that, while economics may be beyond him, education is a subject on which his opinion is as good as anyone else's. In this situation, the teacher is called upon to make sense of the dichotomy which lies at the heart of his role, and to show that strength does not mean repression; that freedom does not mean licence; that mixed-ability teaching does not mean survival of the unfittest; that streaming does not mean the preparation of an academic *herrenvolk* to rule over the rest of us; that generalisations about behavioural controls and classroom methodology are frequently nonsensical. The failure of those who speak for the profession to communicate these truths to the world at large has from time to time exacerbated the difficulties of the ordinary classroom practitioner.

Bearing in mind that teachers are in the business of communication, it is remarkable how poor they are at presenting the truth about themselves. That is because they are actors at heart. Some of the best are hardly real at all, but more like characters from literature, offering remarkable performances not only to children in the classroom but also to their colleagues in the staffroom. It brings a smile to one's lips just to think about some of the people by whom one has been taught or with whom one has worked, and a chill to the heart to think of some others. Were any of them real? Down the years, one begins to wonder.

> One teacher in his time plays many parts.
> At first, probationer, fearful alike
> Of teachers and taught; fearful most of Head,
> On whose opinion swift preferment waits.
> Next, proud possessor of allowances,
> Growing to mark responsibilities
> That make the unpromoted envious,
> Convinced that idle justice sleeps unknowing.
> Now in classroom full of fine confidence,

Sudden and quick in clever repartee,
Fearless in face of devious juvenile,
Seeking the bubble reputation
Even in the cannon's mouth. Then as Head,
Snatched from classroom to be the one who says,
'It shall be thus and thus'; full of wise saws,
But now no longer loved nor understood.
Next comes translation to inspectorate,
Speaking with voice made surer than before
By distance from the fray. Last scene of all,
That ends this strange eventful history,
Is sweet retirement, with tales of children
Good or bad, or in between, remember'd well,
And Friday afternoon deliverance.
So comes surrender to oblivion,
Sans chalk, sans books to mark, sans everything.

A teacher's style of performance will change with the years as his professional skills develop, and from class to class as he adapts to different audiences. Teachers have various conceptions of the purpose of the drama, some believing in containment and others in stimulation. Some are more inclined than others to allow the children to take a significant part in the performance. The regular message of a colleague of mine for one difficult class of fourth-year boys was this: 'Your job is to shut up and listen, and that's *all* it is, got it?' His lessons were orderly, but somewhat lacking in excitement. In the same school, another colleague had a different approach, which he spelled out from time to time to the rest of us in case we cared to learn from him: 'You've got to get the little bastards involved, and never mind the noise.' It was an *apologia* for chaos, but of such a good-natured kind that no one minded unless they happened to be teaching next door. These two polar extremes of attitude provide a rough framework within which to make one kind of analysis of teaching methods. Practitioners all stand somewhere along the line between the shut–'em–up brigade and the let–'em–rip squad. Perhaps the key to real success is never to allow oneself to be pushed by circumstances, or reputation, too far down the line in one direction.

Reputation is not the friend of teachers. Christopher Stace once began a book review: 'It is a well known fact that all schoolmasters are bores, and if it is not a fact, it is a theory advanced by weighty critics, including my sister-in-law Drusilla.' She would not be the only one to attest to the readiness of teachers endlessly to talk about themselves. Where two or three people are gathered together, if there be a teacher among them, he will sooner or later steer the conversation round to what happened at school today. If Chaucer's pilgrims had had a school teacher among them, there never would have been 'The Miller's Tale', 'The Pardoner's Tale', or any other sort of tale except one, for the pedagogue would surely have talked all the way to the holy shrine and back. Teachers are a professional race apart, for lawyers and doctors do not generally behave in this way. What is it about their job which makes the daily reviewing of it such a compulsive activity for those involved?

It is generally believed that a teacher is principally concerned with passing on a body of knowledge. It is assumed that his pupils will be better able to read, write, add up and show command of associated skills at the end of his efforts than at the outset. Children will be expected, after spending between ten and fifteen thousand hours in the education system, to know enough as a result to pass some examinations and go out into the world literate, numerate and employable. In so far as a normally healthy, ordinarily intelligent and reasonably behaved youngster fails to achieve this, he and others will be likely to consider that the education system has defaulted.

But such a simplistic view of the function of a teacher not only falls short of the whole truth, but puts the emphasis in the wrong place. If the passing on of knowledge, and its retention by those receiving it, is the yardstick of good teaching, success is unachievable. Leaving aside command of basic skills, the amount of information offered in the classroom which is likely to be carried into the world beyond is slight. Most adults remember only a small proportion of what they were taught in more than half their subjects at school and we would be surprised were it otherwise. The grand sweep of the history syllabus in a secondary school may mean something to the head of department who devised it, but even his own staff will find it hard to retain much of it. Indeed, each will have his excuse ready when it is discovered that parts are being skipped over: 'Not my period, I'm afraid.'

If one can expect the average child to retain little of what he is taught, how much more is that true of those with learning difficulties? I recollect my own experience on taking over a fourth-year bottom mathematics set one Monday. It being a suitable day for new resolutions and fresh beginnings, the class and I jointly resolved to assume they knew nothing of the rules of multiplication. The assumption was quickly shown to be entirely reasonable, the appalling dimensions of their ignorance being demonstrated with an openness bearing no trace of shame. 'We are', declared a forthright teenage female who was the natural leader of the group, 'no good at maths.'

By Tuesday little progress had been made, but on Wednesday the light began to dawn for a few. By dint of slow persistence, a good deal had been achieved by the penultimate day of the week and on Friday one or two were even heard to say things like: 'Sir, it's easy really, ennit?' But it was a siren call, destined to fetch me up on the rocks of unwarranted optimism. At the end of a long weekend of televisual traumas and disco delights, the class assembled on another Monday morning, grumbling once again that they were no good at maths. And so it proved, for those rules upon which they had but a few days earlier placed a finger-tip grasp had slipped away. It was as if the previous week's lessons had never taken place. So we began again. My fears that the class would be bored by the repetition were groundless, for most of them did not recognise that they were going over the same ground as before, so dim was their recollection of my recent efforts with them.

Such experiences are the daily bread of those who teach slow learners, especially in the area of mathematics, in which it is socially acceptable to remain forever incompetent. At the end of it all, after years of striving, the youngsters concerned leave school possessed of little more by way of knowledge than when they arrived. Seeing that one of the principal responsibilities of the teaching profession must surely be towards those who find learning difficult, the implications are profound. It is at least arguable that those boys and girls who are naturally good at learning are less in need of highly trained teachers than youngsters with learning problems. The very justification for a teaching profession must be that, without it, children will fail to learn. Thus, the more likely they are to fail, the more needful the attentions of the teacher. And yet, educational success in this country is most usually measured not by what is achieved with those who find learning hard but by what is achieved by those who find it easy. Here is a paradox which gives food for thought.

What such thought reveals is that the principal responsibility of a teacher has less to do with the passing on of information than is generally assumed. Since so many will retain so little, the whole exercise must be a monumental waste of time if retained knowledge is its purpose.

But the activity in which a teacher is actually engaged is passing on himself. It is not what he teaches that matters most, but what he is as a person. If any reader doubts it, let him look back to his own education and ask himself what he remembers. It will not be the material he was taught, but a few of the people who did the teaching. They will have left their mark upon him. The Zulus have an apposite proverb: 'I cannot hear a word you are saying, for what you *are* shouts so loudly in my ears.'

Herein resides an awful truth for all who teach and rear the young: the principal effect of what we do is bound up with children's readiness to imitate. The story is told of a young man entering the profession by way of a post at a state secondary school. Tall of stature and immaculate in appearance, he was known to be a distinguished sportsman. His dark blazer with dazzling white handkerchief spilling from the breast pocket, carefully creased grey slacks, highly polished shoes and club tie marked him out in juvenile eyes as someone special. After a week or two of his being in charge of a class of admiring first-year boys, it was noted that most had taken to having white handkerchiefs spilling from the breast pockets of their school blazers.

Young people are much given to imitating the dress and mannerisms of those they respect and admire. More important, a teacher's values are also up for consideration. They are either adopted or rejected, depending not upon their efficacy but upon the observer's opinion of the person holding them. George Farquhar was right three centuries ago: 'We love the precepts for the teacher's sake.' So there comes, pat, like the catastrophe of the old comedy, the truth about the nature of a teacher's role. He deals most importantly not in knowledge, but values; and the values are his own.

If it is true that what teaching is about is not what at first appears, the same applies to schools. They are places in which things are rarely as they at first seem. 'Summerhill', wrote the great A. S. Neill in his book of that title, 'runs along without any authority or obedience.' His splendid Suffolk institution, established in 1921 to give children a unique kind of education in self-government, will forever be regarded as the first great experiment in educational libertarianism in this country. And yet, despite the director's declared opposition to authority and obedience, he found no difficulty in making very clear rules in the school prospectus on the subject of clothing for pupils. 'Parents', he uncompromisingly asserted, 'should not send white shirts, sweaters or socks, they get dirty too soon.' There was one particularly strict regulation: 'The telephone is a private one and pupils are not allowed to use it.' A special note was added for transatlantic clients: 'American parents please note, our time is at least five hours ahead of yours, and if you suddenly want to speak to us at 10 p.m. in New York, we have to get up at 3 a.m. to answer.' The need for this request was underlined in a letter I received from Neill in June 1973, which must have been one of the last he wrote before his death. He had ten days earlier published his life story, *Neill, Neill, Orange Peel* and, at nearly ninety, felt too damned tired to write any more. He observed that Summerhill had a waiting list a yard long, 'mostly furriners'. Thus did Summerhill become a place in the countryside of East Anglia at which a Scotsman provided a special type of education for American children. Neither that, nor Neill's readiness to make rules when they were necessary, line up with the general conception of Summerhill. The same could be said for most schools: their public image is inclined to be at some distance from the reality.

It is a fact of which two groups of people need to take special note, *viz* parents and newcomers to the teaching profession. Any parent choosing a school for a child needs to make sure that what the school says it is doing is actually happening inside its walls, and that what public report declares to be the school's position in the educational spectrum is borne out in its classrooms. Equally, any young teacher looking for the right place at which to begin a teaching career needs to take some trouble to find out what is the true ethos of any school under consideration. A head teacher in search of a physicist is likely to represent his institution in terms which would make the Clarendon Laboratory sound like a withdrawal unit for slow learners. That would be generally regarded as defensible on the grounds that it is the head teacher's job to staff his school effectively by whatever means he can and that any ambition he may have to establish a good science department will hang upon his acquiring the best available teachers.

It is no condemnation of schools to say that they are not what they sometimes appear to be. A school is not a petrified edifice but an evolving organism, in a constant state of change. From inside any organisation, it is not always easy to discern the point of development which has been reached or how far the leadership has drifted from its intended course. A salutary warning hangs on the wall of BBC Broadcasting House in London:

> This temple of the arts and muses is dedicated to Almighty God by the first governors . . . and they pray that good seed sown may bring forth good harvest, that all things foul and hostile to peace may be banished hence, and that the people, inclining their ear to whatsoever things are lovely and honest, whatsoever things are of good report, may tread the path of virtue and of wisdom.

Should we laugh or weep to be reminded of the use to which Lord Reith and his fellow governors thought broadcasting would be put? But then, what one claims today by way of intention or reputation is rarely likely to apply tomorrow. 'There is', wrote Philip Jordan in *The Guardian* in the autumn of 1980, 'a tenet in television that a reputation lasts for twice as many years as it took to establish it.' What is true of broadcasting organisations applies no less to schools, whose reputations are frequently out of phase with reality.

There are two realisations which someone needs to grasp if he or she is considering teaching as a career. They are ones which all who are concerned with education – parents, experienced practitioners, politicians and others – might do well to bear in mind.

Firstly, a teacher is unique. There is no other profession in which the responsibilities are as impossible to postpone. The group of children he has to teach cannot be placed in a pending basket if he is absent. If he is just five minutes late for his rendezvous with them, there may well be chaos, calling for the intervention of a colleague. Walking from one classroom to another, a teacher bears responsibility for the behaviour of the children he passes on the way. Should he and his colleagues deny that responsibility, they are likely to pay for it in terms of children's classroom attitudes. Traditionally, teachers have also accepted a share of the responsibility for the behaviour, safety and welfare of children both inside and outside the school building during breaks in teaching. The effects of their opting out of that responsibility in the sixties and seventies are to be seen in lower general standards of behaviour in some schools. The very fact that teachers have in the past been regarded as the guardians of their pupils from the moment they enter the school gates in the morning until the time of their passing through them again at the end of the day underlines the uniqueness of the teacher's role.

No other profession places such burdens as these upon its members. The houseman in a hospital is not held responsible for setting the tone of the institution in which he serves. Should he so wish, he may simply get on with treating his own patients and ignore everything else which is going on. A general practitioner is not required to control the behaviour of the people in his waiting room while at the same time attempting to treat someone in his surgery. A lawyer is not held to have done less than his duty simply by losing a case. But teachers are expected to accept a part in setting the overall ethos of their schools; to handle up to thirty disparate individuals all at the same time; to achieve academic success with those in their charge. Never has so much been expected of one group of human beings by the rest.

The second realisation which needs to be made is that what

appears impossible is achievable. That is an important message for every probationer teacher to grasp, for there are few human experiences more difficult, exhausting and likely to generate self-doubt than one's first twelve months as a full-time classroom practitioner. 'Nothing on God's earth could have prepared me for this,' said one young woman after her first three weeks of what she called real teaching. It occurred to me at the time, and still does, that she was making two points, *viz* that teacher training can do no more than hint at classroom reality and that a teacher needs to look beyond the things of this world for the resources to cope.

The apparent impossibility of the teacher's function is not difficult to illustrate. Consider a young man or woman of twenty-two in front of a comprehensive class of teenagers. While some will be keen to learn, a fair number will have no enthusiasm for the academic process. There will be two or three whose distaste for learning is militant. Some will have less ability than the rest, while others will have such problems at home or in their private lives as to distract their minds beyond all thought of learning. One or two will very likely be thinking about their next court appearance or appointment with a social worker. Almost certainly, the attitudes of the hostile, preoccupied and least able will dominate the classroom at the outset. Only if the young teacher is able to overcome them will it prove possible to draw upon the keenness of the few and the readiness of the majority to acquiescence. At first, success will appear beyond reach. When it begins to emerge, the young teacher may well regard it as a miracle. But later, it will seem a matter of course. John Donne has an apposite comment:

> There is nothing that God hath established in a constant course of nature, and which therefore is done every day, but would seem a miracle, and exercise our admiration, if it were done but once . . . only the daily doing takes off the admiration.

Everyone knows about teachers. Or do they? This chapter has attempted to establish a general basis for considering the activity in which a teacher is involved. A closer examination of the subject involves scrutiny of such things as a teacher's duties and responsibilities, the means by which someone enters the profession, the settlement of salaries and so on. These and other issues are dealt with in the chapters which follow. Since many of them are complex, giving rise to problems which frequently seem insoluble, it is all too easy to lose sight of fundamentals. It is the need for teachers to be regarded as professionals, and for them to conduct themselves to that end, that has led me to embark upon a new career and to write this book.

In his infamous reference to teachers, George Bernard Shaw simply labelled them as the greatest dropouts of all: 'He who can, does. He who cannot, teaches.' Sadly, there remains some justification for that description. Will a new identity for teachers emerge during the eighties? There are forces at work to establish genuine professionalism in the ranks of those who teach; there are others that promise to reduce teachers to the educational equivalent of factory hands. The question of which it is to be will almost certainly be settled once and for all in this decade.

Two

The Question of Duties

In England and Wales, it is a matter of surprise to many outside the teaching profession, and to not a few inside it, that the statutory machinery which exists for the settlement of teachers' salaries is not matched by any similar arrangement for deciding what they are supposed to do for their money. As a result, definition of a teacher's duties is chiefly remarkable for its absence; voluntariness is the basis of a whole range of activities which most teachers regularly perform as a matter of course.

The conditions of service upon which local education authorities and the teachers' unions have found it possible to agree are set down in what is known as the Burgundy Book. It deals with such matters as how salaries shall be paid, arrangements for taking leave of absence, grievance procedures and so on. It also outlines the main provisions of the law with regard to such things as redundancy payments, unfair dismissal and sex discrimination. All teachers should be acquainted with the Burgundy Book, a copy of which ought properly to be available in every school maintained by a local education authority. Its provisions are, according to the foreword, 'the accepted practice of the day-to-day teacher/employer relationship'. That being so, the following entries become all the more significant:

Teacher's Day
No existing collective agreement

Teacher's Duties
No existing collective agreement

The forum within which collective agreements on teachers' conditions of service are made or not made is a non-statutory *ad hoc* body called into being by the local education authorities and known as CLEA/ST, indicating that it brings together members of the Council of Local Education Authorities and representatives of school teachers. Why is it this forum has failed to agree the nature and extent of a teacher's duties? Because the two sides have different motives for discussing the subject. The employers are concerned to give as much definition as possible to the obligations of a teacher, in order to know what may and may not be insisted upon. The teachers on the other hand are concerned to keep definition to a minimum in order to be able to make their own rules and interpret them as they see fit. There is much more readiness on one side than the other even to discuss the subject, the enthusiasm of employers being regarded by some teachers' leaders as a case of Brer Fox inviting Brer Rabbit over for a bit of a chat.

The ability of a teacher to argue, should he or she so wish, that a particular activity is undertaken from goodwill touches on every aspect of school life outside the classroom. There is no specific statutory or contractual obligation to attend staff meetings beyond school hours or to meet with parents when they are available in the evenings to discuss their children's work and progress. Teachers cannot be required to give up any part of their extensive holidays for in-service training, planning of the curriculum, staff conferences or things of that kind. How much importance a teacher attaches to lesson preparation and marking is a matter for him or her to decide, as is the amount of time devoted to them. There are those who categorically refuse to attend to them beyond normal school hours, while others spend their lives creating visual aids and correcting exercises.

Of course, the effectiveness of an individual's teaching does not necessarily correlate with readiness to attend staff meetings, go on courses, build elaborate teaching aids or be surrounded by exercise books from corn flake to cocoa time. Indeed, enthusiasm for these things may mask incompetence. I once knew a teacher of foreign languages whose extensive entries in his pupils' exercise books, inscribed in the most careful copperplate handwriting, were a beauty to behold. Rarely was he seen without his red pen in his hand, converting ordinary exercises into highly decorated works of art. He once confessed that marking was all he cared for. 'But', he added, 'the little sods never read any of it.' In fact, his teaching ability was slight, and his classroom performance a daily disaster. But he had found a way of escape, a means of discovering some small degree of contentment.

The fact that different teachers spend vastly differing amounts of time on such activities as those described serves to underline the fact that they are voluntary in extent if not nature and that no one is obliged to take them very seriously. When one turns to the question of supervisory duties, the sense of obligation varies even more greatly between one teacher and the next.

Supervision of all kinds has been the subject of intense debate for many years. Whether or not a teacher must undertake dinner duties, playground duties, wet-break duties, school-gate duties, corridor-patrol duties, guardianship of fire alarms and toilets (comprehensive schools), guardianship of the squash courts (selective schools), guardianship of the polo pitch (public schools), is more or less questionable within the proper meaning of that term. That is to say, while there is no doubt what the answers are in some of the areas named, opinions vary in others.

It might seem that, whatever else depends upon goodwill, a teacher is at least required actually to teach when available in school and free to do so. But the refusal of teachers to give up what are known as free periods to cover for absent colleagues is now common.

It is unlikely that those outside the school system fully appreciate the significance of teachers being unprepared to take their col-leagues' classes when they are away. When John Mays researched into the operation of a Merseyside comprehensive from a base in the University of Liverpool Department of Social Science, cover arrange-ments came to him as a revelation, as is shown by this passage from his book *School of Tomorrow*:

A particularly interesting feature of the school is the system of 'subbing': substituting for absent members of staff. With a large staff absences are fairly common. Moreover, the wide range of outside activities carried on by the school, the camps and visits to places of interest, and the fact that senior members of staff are given time off to make contact with parents, means that there can be as many as ten teachers away at any one time. The sub list, consisting of those who are expected to take the classes of absentee members of staff, is sent round to the house blocks before nine in the morning. The system works efficiently but because of its impersonal nature and the fact that it can mean the loss of coveted free periods produces a fair amount of mild criticism.

Criticism of having to cover for one another is less mild among teachers than it was when those words were written at the end of the sixties. There should be, it is now argued, a permanent body of supply teachers employed by every local education authority to stand in for those absent through sickness, away on courses or off on school journeys. He who would have his pupils climb every mountain and ford every stream should be replaced in the classroom by some better method than one which requires other members of staff with no taste for rocky crags or babbling brooks to do the job he is most obviously paid for.

Not that every teacher worries about the loss of what John Mays describes as coveted free periods, since there are those who are not accustomed to having any. While regarded in secondary schools as a fundamental right, which would have been written into the Magna Carta had any of the barons at Runnymede been awake to his real responsibilities, they are not often found at primary level. Education is littered with paradoxes, and none is more glaring than the assumption that, while teachers in secondary schools need recovery time built into their timetables, those in junior and infant schools may be quite happily left in the company of pupils all day long. Some would say the ordering of things should be exactly the other way round. While it is not too difficult for someone teaching teenagers to set them work during lessons in order to take a breather, it is about a thousand miles the other side of possibility with five-year-olds. The existing situation has come about not by design but historical accident, having to do with the fact that primary schools are descended from public elementary schools while secondary schools are the heirs of the grammar school tradition.

Perhaps it is time for the consequences of history to be properly examined.

Cover arrangements that fail to give special consideration to probationers threaten their competence at a time when they need the best possible conditions for mastering what Michael Marland rightly calls the craft of the classroom. New teachers inevitably have difficulty in coming to terms with the physical, mental and emotional demands of timetable commitments that go well beyond anything experienced in training. To be faced with the loss of non-teaching time, or to be provided with little or none of it, saps the will of the most starry-eyed recruit to the professional ranks.

Since the maintenance of discipline, which is always the new arrival's greatest worry, requires a considerable effort of will, the knock-on effect of cover arrangements that make heavy demands on probationers is all too clear. Happily, the problem is recognised more than once it was, and those entering the profession in the eighties receive more consideration than those who went before. Indeed, readiness to share the problems of the probationer and to offer sympathy and support, is a hallmark of the new generation of experienced practitioners. This happy outcome of staffroom egalitarianism counterbalances some of its other results.

When Alistair Cooke rose to speak at Guildhall some years ago, he expressed himself honoured to stand where Churchill had stood and where Charles James Fox had frequently fallen. To be associated with those who have lost their balance is not necessarily less honourable than to follow in the footsteps of those who have managed to maintain theirs. Thus it is that most teachers are at one with their colleagues who have discipline problems and often feel more at home with them than with those who seem to have a natural talent for handling juveniles whose delinquent acts make the Artful Dodger look like the male equivalent of Snow White. There is therefore a great deal of sympathy among experienced teachers for the sort of situation facing many newcomers to the profession as a result of cover arrangements.

But objection to covering does not only stem from the pressures arising from having to do one's own job and someone else's as well. The very prospect of covering some classes has been known to strike terror into a teacher's heart. I recollect a young physicist who had a hard time of it with his own classes. Entering his laboratory one day, I enquired why one of his third formers was climbing out of the window. 'Actually,' came the embarrassed explanation, 'he's climbing back in.' When this young newcomer to schoolmastering was one morning found to be the only available person to cover a fourth-year RE lesson, the whole staffroom held its breath. The man himself, on being delivered of the news, disappeared into the gents and locked himself away. At morning break he had to be enticed out with promises of tea and biscuits and no headmasterly retribution.

The nature and extent of the duties a teacher may be called upon to perform in any of the areas so far discussed have never been defined. The law of the land and the kind of contract issued to most teachers by local education authorities do, however, provide a basis for discussing whether or not performance really does depend entirely upon goodwill.

The 1944 Education Act made it mandatory for local education authorities to draw up articles of government for their schools describing the separate functions to be exercised in the running of them by the three principal parties involved, *viz* head teachers, school governors and the local education authority itself. The duties that in consequence fall to a head teacher are normally based on model articles issued by the Ministry of Education in 1945. These state that he or she 'shall control the internal organisation, management and discipline of the school, shall exercise supervision over the teaching and non-teaching staff, and shall have the power of suspending pupils.' Since it would be beyond the competence of any single person to carry out all these responsibilities personally, participation by others is tacitly assumed.

That assumption is spelled out in the contracts that are issued by local education authorities to those they employ to teach in their schools. A teacher currently practising in the maintained sector is likely to hold a contract based upon principles laid down in the *Schools Regulations* that have been in force for a quarter of a century. These state that a teacher must be employed under a written agreement which shall 'either expressly, or by reference to specified regulations or minutes, define the conditions of service'. What those conditions shall be is left to local education authorities, no restriction being placed upon what may be demanded of a teacher except that he 'shall not be required to perform any duties except such as are connected with the work of the school or to abstain outside the school hours from any occupations which do not interfere with the due performance of his duties.' The more one regards the first half of that passage, the less it looks like any sort of constraint upon what a teacher may be called upon to do. A typical form of words arising from the regulations is that used in Nottinghamshire: 'An assistant teacher shall act under the control of, and in accordance with the directions of, the Headteacher and shall carry out such duties as are assigned to him or her.' The only limitation placed upon what may be expected is that laid down in the old *Schools Regulations* quoted above, the relevant passage being employed *verbatim* in the Nottinghamshire contract.

It is not clear what significance should be attached to the fact that the *Education (Schools and Further Education) Regulations 1981* and the *Education (Teachers) Regulations 1982,* which have superseded the old *Schools Regulations 1959,* make no mention of the principles that have in the past applied. While existing contracts are not affected, and while local education authorities may well continue to use the old form of words in the future, it is an open question whether reference to duties may disappear from contracts after a while. Whether or not that will amount to anything of consequence remains to be seen.

As things stand at present, a teacher's contract makes nonsense of a good deal of what has already been said in this chapter, not to mention the discussions which have taken place over the years between local education authorities and the teachers' unions. There would seem little need for reliance on a teacher's goodwill, and even less for any attempt to specify by national collective agreement what are and what are not a teacher's duties. A head teacher may call upon a member of staff to do anything at all, provided it has to do with the work of the school.

But the road which is laid by the hardcore of school articles of government and the chippings of teachers' contracts is a bumpy one, full of potholes. What appears to be a smooth surface from a distance looks quite different to those who travel on it. That is because of two factors which are at work. Firstly, to every action carried out by a head teacher there has to be applied the test of reasonableness. Secondly, the head teacher of today, in attempting to run a school, is involved in what is essentially a political activity: he or she practises the art of the possible. In short, those responsibilities which a teacher stands ready to assume without question or argument depend not upon contract or statute, but upon the skill of the head teacher in managing his staff.

The statements which give control of a school and its staff to the head teacher do no more than provide a framework within which the allocation of duties and responsibilities may effectively be made. At his peril will a head call upon his staff to undertake what is unreasonable. That applies not only to the areas of activity already described in this chapter, which have had to do for the most part with what happens outside the classroom, but also the most important feature of all in a school's organisation: the allocation of classes on the regular timetable.

The chronic shortage of mathematics specialists often makes it necessary for head teachers to persuade non-specialists to help out from time to time. As often as not in my own experience, the only available person on the staff turns out to be a geographer or historian who is proud of being innumerate. That is not an insult to those who teach geography and history, for mathematical incompetence is entirely acceptable in the teaching profession in this country, as it is in the population at large. Indeed, not being able to add up for toffee is a form of intellectual snobbery. Inability to recognise Beethoven's Ninth Symphony or to understand the fool in *King Lear* is, on the other hand, a sign of a gravely inadequate education and upbringing. Cajoling a non-specialist into teaching mathematics may therefore call upon all a head teacher's diplomatic skills. It may be necessary to exercise a mixture of flattery ('I know you have a broad view of the curriculum and can handle anything, Mr Jones'), bribery ('Have I received your application for the Scale 2 with responsibility for lost property?') and subtle appeals to the darker side of staffroom relationships ('Mr Smith will be furious when he knows I have offered you his favourite class').

More seriously, a head teacher must base his claim for assistance on reason. Thus, while asking a physicist to help out with lower school mathematics is worth a try and could as a last resort be insisted upon, asking a linguist to teach physics to the fifth is not and could not. Knowing what to ask, what not to ask, and in what circumstances a request may become an instruction, is the key to success. Using the head teacher's power to direct and control what happens as the normal basis for every decision about teaching arrangements is likely to create a situation in which a school loses its direction and a head teacher his control. The name of the game is consensus. The words of Harold Macmillan are apposite: 'Quiet, calm deliberation disentangles every knot.'

If these things be true in the matter of timetable allocation, they have even more obvious implications for all those duties and responsibilities outside the classroom which teachers regard as voluntary in the final analysis. Here, reasonableness alone is not enough; it is the art of the possible which holds sway. Thus, while it may seem perfectly reasonable to ask the staff of a school to give up a Saturday afternoon to help with the summer fête, it may not be possible to persuade all to do so. In that event, there is nothing to be done, despite the statement in a teacher's contract that the only duties he or she may not be required to perform are ones unconnected with the work of the school.

The accepted duties of a teacher outside the classroom are in the event determined by custom and practice. There is great variation from school to school, reflecting the different ways in which they operate. In his book *Fifteen Thousand Hours*, Michael Rutter identifies as the key to understanding a school an appreciation of its ethos as a social institution. He argues that no one particular ethos or style is necessarily more successful than another; but for lack of a coherent and identifiable way of doing things, a school will fail. Part of the style of any school is the pattern of duties and responsibilities undertaken by the staff as a result of accepted custom and practice. Thus, it may be that a particular school places heavy emphasis on supervision of the premises when the children are not in class, with the result that a good deal of patrolling of playgrounds and corridors is regarded as the norm for any teacher. In another school, leaving children free of supervision to explore the boundaries of human experience may be seen as good education, so staff will be called upon to perform fewer supervisory duties.

The establishment of a particular pattern in any school will depend upon a variety of factors. The head teacher will have his own ideas about the style he or she wishes to create, but there will be other influences at work, of which two require mention. Firstly, if the dominant personalities in the staffroom are at one with the leadership, success becomes more rather than less likely. Conversely, if there is a significant body of influential teachers with a different view of things, there is likely to be something of a battle over the duties to be performed. Secondly, if the trade union presence is supportive of the leadership, the signs are good. If not, the head teacher is in trouble.

The question which duties a teacher should accept and which reject is frequently brought to the centre of the stage in a school when a new head teacher is appointed. That is because he or she is likely to bring a new style, calling for a review of existing arrangements. The attitude of some teachers to doing things differently from before makes the introduction of flexible rostering on the railways look like a smooth operation. It is at a time of change that people are most likely to examine closely the whole range of activities in which they have been involved. The arrival of a new head teacher is make-up-your-mind-time for staff who may have been quietly reconsidering their position for weeks, months or years. The story is told of a newly-appointed primary head who, having been assured by his predecessor that he was inheriting a splendid staff who would do just anything they were asked, turned up to find they had without exception decided to call it a day so far as duties in the lunch hour were concerned.

Calling it a day on duties which once attached to particular subjects has also become common. No longer may a head teacher take it for granted that a music specialist will sacrifice his private life in order to run the choir, train the orchestra, conduct concerts and so on. Nor may he assume that teachers of physical education will give up their Saturdays to travel with school teams and referee matches. On appointing people to salaried posts of special responsibility, head teachers are getting into the habit of making out-of-school activities part of the deal. But that serves merely to make it more likely that teachers on the basic scale will opt out, on the grounds that they would be fools to do for nothing what someone else gets paid for. Of course, there are still a great many teachers who give up huge quantities of their own time to their pupils without thinking twice about being paid for it; but the climate is changing.

It cannot be without significance that, in the one area where there once existed a statutory requirement that certain duties be carried out, it has been removed. Until 1968, teachers were required by regulations made under the authority of the 1944 Education Act to assist in the supervision of children taking school meals. The working party whose findings changed the situation said in its report that its principal aim was to find a way of abolishing the requirement that teachers should supervise 'while continuing to provide adequately for the safety and welfare of children during the midday break'. The solution was seen in terms of making dinner duties voluntary, and bringing in paid ancillaries to cover the gaps which would consequently arise. The report of the working party appears as the first appendix at the end of this book. But anyone who thought the recommendations made in 1968 and accepted by the Secretary of State would once and for all resolve the problem of midday supervision was doomed to disappointment. There were two reasons.

Firstly, the assumption that ancillaries would be capable of supervising children of all ages and attitudes as effectively as teachers was false. The representatives of the teachers' unions on the working party must have been well aware of it, but they were concerned to have their members released from the obligation to supervise by whatever means fell to hand. It would in fact have been an unhappy reflection upon the profession had it turned out that ancillaries in general could handle large numbers of children just as well as their teachers. Where dinner ladies have shown themselves so capable, people have been led to wonder about the special skills the profession claims for its members. The same would be true in the field of medicine if untrained casuals had shown themselves able to take care of hospital patients as effectively as nurses. However, in general, the story of ancillary staff looking after the condition of a school during the lunch period is not a happy one.

Secondly, that part of the 1968 agreement relating to the head teacher has proved entirely unworkable. Here again, the teachers' representatives on the working party must have known it would be so, and it is astonishing that the head teacher members allowed themselves to be railroaded into including provisions that were mutually irreconcilable. Under the revised arrangements introduced in 1968, a teacher may withdraw entirely from midday duties and leave the school premises for the whole of the lunch period. In many schools – especially primary schools – every member of staff except the head teacher does just that. Some union representatives positively encourage it, so that there can be no question about their members' rejection of responsibilities of any kind. In face of this, the proviso that the head teacher should, like everyone else, be able to enjoy a proper and satisfactory break in which he can relax and rest and, if he wishes, leave the school premises, is nonsense. It is made especially so by an accompanying reminder that he must retain overall responsibility for the school during the midday break. With no other teachers on the premises, who is to carry out that responsibility if he pushes off to the Nagging Head? To add insult to injury, the working party clearly stated that there was 'a professional responsibility on the teaching staff as a whole' to support the head teacher at midday with regard both to the conduct of the school meal and to general supervision. That has been ignored in many schools, since it so obviously contradicts the whole point of the main findings of the working party. Any head teacher or local education authority attempting to insist on all teachers honouring that particular part of the 1968 agreement would be doomed to failure.

As a result, a huge burden has been thrown on head teachers and those of their colleagues who are prepared to accept the full implications of the 1968 report, rather than just the negative parts. It was, of course, hoped by the Secretary of State that everyone would do just that. His agreement to change existing arrangements was given in the belief that both teachers and local education authorities had entered into an undertaking to give their fullest support (*sic*) to the recommendations which had been made. But no such undertaking has been fulfilled; nor was it ever the intention of some of those involved that it should be. The consequence is spelled out by Geoffrey Barrell, author of *Teachers and the Law,* in a leaflet published by the Professional Association of Teachers:

> In those schools where a majority of the staff have placed the emphasis on their need for a proper and satisfactory break, the head and those of his colleagues who have seen it as their professional responsibility to maintain the school meals service have frequently found themselves doing dinner duty every day. This was clearly not the intention of the working party.
>
> (*Midday Supervision*, January 1982)

The only part of that statement one might feel inclined to question is the last sentence. While the working party as a whole doubtless assumed that all teachers would help to keep the school ship afloat for the midday period, it seems likely that some of the more astute members were well aware that many teachers would be prepared to let it sink. The water is already lapping at the gunwales.

The attempt to clarify teachers' responsibilities has enabled those so disposed to abdicate from them completely. Perhaps that is why the government has been so reluctant to press on with attempts to come to terms with the conditions of service issue. Better that everything be left as vague and uncertain as possible, since there is bound to be a sufficient amount of goodwill here and there in the profession to see things through.

But there has been one serious attempt made by the government to sort out the relationship between salaries and conditions. On 22 January 1981, the then Secretary of State for Education and Science sent draft proposals to the teachers' unions for amending the Remuneration of Teachers Act of 1965. Mark Carlisle's covering letter spoke of his wish to review the existing legislation 'with a view to establishing new unified national negotiating machinery'. His principal intention was to replace the Burnham Committee with a body responsible for determining both the salaries and the conditions of service of teachers in primary and secondary schools.

The full proposals appear in the second appendix to this book.

At a meeting on 25 March 1981 at the Department of Education and Science, the leaders of all the teachers' unions met the Secretary of State and his mandarins to discuss what was proposed. The Professional Association of Teachers expressed support in principle, giving as grounds the irrationality of continuing to ignore the question of what a teacher was supposed to do while attempting to settle what he or she should be paid for doing it. But the big battalions were opposed to change. At the close of the meeting, there was a discussion between the Minister and his civil servants about whether a new document should be produced in the light of what had been said. My notes record: 'Mark Carlisle and his advisers were not agreed about this.' One suspects they were not agreed about raising the subject of unified machinery in the first place. The prospect of such a dramatic change in existing arrangements was a fearful one for the educational bureaucracy to contemplate.

On 30 June 1981, the Secretary of State was asked in a Parliamentary Question whether he held to his intention to amend the Remuneration of Teachers Act 1965. He replied: 'Yes. It is the Government's intention to amend the Act so as to bring pay and other conditions of service within the scope of a single negotiating body. I have however come to the conclusion, following consultations with the major parties concerned, that it would be right to consider further some aspects of my proposals for legislation.'

Whether Mark Carlisle actually meant to press ahead with his plans one will never know. The question became irrelevant with his departure to the back benches in September 1981. With the arrival of Sir Keith Joseph at the Department of Education and Science, the impetus to bring about unified negotiating machinery disappeared like vintage port at an All Souls dinner. The new Secretary of State quickly made clear his lack of enthusiasm for statutory change. Early in 1982, the Under Secretary of State with responsibility for schools, in the person of Dr Rhodes Boyson, repeated the message, adding his personal view that contractual definition of a teacher's duties would mean the end of teaching as a profession.

But events in the spring of 1982 drew attention to the dangers of leaving unresolved a problem which, for lack of a solution, made it possible for the most militant elements in the profession to bring the education system to a halt with astonishing ease and without their making the slightest sacrifice, except of their pupils. Child sacrifice as a means of appeasement being somewhat outmoded, there was a general stirring of the national conscience, and mutterings here and there in the corridors of power that it was time something was done. As a consequence, it may well be that a teacher's duties are nearer to some kind of statutory or contractual definition than ever before. Those who believe, like Leon Trotsky, that war is the locomotive of history, will not be surprised to hear it.

War was first declared in the late seventies. It was then that teachers first realised what kind of weapon lay unused in their negotiating armoury. Because such a wide area of teachers' activities could, one way or another, to this or that extent, in the absence of any national collective agreement, be declared voluntary, their ability to damage and disrupt without cost to themselves was enormous. As long as this weaponry was not used, no one worried too much about its existence. But in 1982, the missiles were paraded and fired. In the salary negotiations of that year, the strategy first recommended by the most militant of the teachers' unions, the National Association of Schoolmasters/Union of Women Teachers (NAS/UWT), was quickly taken up by the National Union of Teachers (NUT). A most significant development came when these two unions were joined by the previously moderate Assistant Masters and Mistresses Association (AMMA) in a withdrawal of goodwill.

Withdrawal from midday supervision and from meetings out of school hours, plus withdrawal from covering for teachers absent for more than one day in the case of the NAS/UWT, had an effect which went well beyond children going without school dinners and parents losing the opportunity to discuss their children's work with school staff. Up and down the country, children turned off school premises during the lunch break went on the rampage. In Harrogate, of all places, extra police were drafted in 'to keep an eye on gangs of children in the town centre during the dispute' (*Yorkshire Evening Post*). One head teacher wrote: 'The reputation it has taken our school years to establish in the neighbourhood has been destroyed in a week.' A story was told of a school in Lincolnshire where, with everyone off the premises at midday, the children got into the main teaching block and locked the teachers out of afternoon school. Some head teachers decided not to attempt to open up again in the afternoons after closing down at midday and so teaching time was lost. Teenagers making final preparations for their public examinations became desperate, as did their parents. One rang to ask: 'What on earth is the teaching profession doing to our children?'

Given that invigilation of public examinations depends a great deal on teachers' goodwill, the prospect was grim. A GCE paper does not stop for the lunch hour, nor conveniently come to an end with the four o'clock bell. Unless teachers are prepared to work outside normal lesson hours the whole invigilation system collapses, as it does if they are unprepared to give up those coveted free periods John Mays writes about. As spring makes way for early summer, life in a secondary school comes to be dominated by the public examination system.Like the monster Leviathan, it is king over all, and many are laid low by it. The member of staff to whom responsibility is given for keeping the situation under some kind of control ages visibly as the examination weeks go by. Bringing the right group of pupils together for the right papers at the right time and ensuring that all is safely handed out and safely gathered in is hard enough. Ensuring that the staff turn up to invigilate is sometimes even more difficult, calling for organisational skill, sophisticated diplomacy and the faith of an anchorite. That is because the public examinations change a school's normal arrangements – a phenomenon to which teachers find it hard to adjust. When you have always taught your fifth-year history class period three on a Thursday, it is hard to remember you are free of that and have instead to go and invigilate biology period four when you would normally be in the staffroom reading *The Times Educational Supplement* or explaining to colleagues why the head should take early retirement. Anyone who throws a disruptive spanner into the works of summer examination arrangements adds confusion to confusion and seriously threatens children's prospects in a way not possible at other times of the school year. A leading spokesman for one teachers' union knew just what kind of threat he was presenting when, in the spring of 1982, he spelled out the implications of the withdrawal of goodwill which was in prospect: 'It will be the greatest disruption of the examination system this country has ever seen.' (*Daily Telegraph*, 25 March 1982)

The debacle of 1982, which led the arbitrators to whom the salary dispute was eventually referred to urge both sides to review the way in which they conducted their affairs, brought local education authorities near to the point of desperation in their desire to settle the question of teachers' duties. The unions, however, were no more enthusiastic than they had ever been to co-operate in giving contractual definition to their members' responsibilities. Feelings spilled over into the Burnham Committee in February 1983 when Alistair Lawton, the leader of the management side, opened up his response to the teachers' 1983 salary claim with an astonishing tirade on the failure of teachers to fulfil a promise 'that they would meet to discuss matters other than Burnham'. It would, he insisted, be 'a very big mistake of teachers throughout the country to underestimate the effect of this continued frustration of employers' views'.

There will continue to be deep fears and suspicions within the teaching profession of specification of hours, tasks and responsibilities for two principal reasons. Firstly, specification could prove to be a freedom charter for the idler and artful dodger. For example, minimum hours will quickly be translated into maximum hours by the least committed. As the offspring of a newspaper worker, I was able as a student to secure a holiday job in Fleet Street. Mine was a humble task, pushing a trolley from one place to another. Keen to show my worth, I ignored what was known as the washing-up bell at five to six on my first day, trundling onwards to the end of the warehouse instead of stopping forthwith. There came a tap on my shoulder. Here was none other than the father of the chapel: 'Push that trolley one more yard,' said he, 'and you won't set foot in this place again.' So much for the attitudes which go with job specification. Teachers reading this will know which of their colleagues will be the shoulder-tappers when four o'clock is knocking-off time in the contract.

Secondly, it is the essence of professionalism that one *chooses* how

long to spend on the job; how to carry out one's general responsibilities in special situations; when to come and when to go; when to be
in a certain place and when not; what matters and what does not
matter. Conversely, it is the antithesis of professionalism to be told
what to do; when to do it; how to do it. Taken too far, specification
of a teacher's duties will turn him into a lackey.

Some politicians and administrators would wish to place teachers
in precisely that position. If it is true that schools would be much
easier to run if it were not for children, it is equally the case that
officialdom would find the education system far more manageable if
it were not for the teaching profession. In so far as tighter
restrictions on teachers might mean more power for those who
would not know one end of a school from the other, it must be
regarded with suspicion.

There is, therefore, a paradox facing all those concerned with
improving the quality of schooling in this country. While the time
would seem to have arrived when clearer definition of a teacher's
duties seems necessary, there is need for the whole question to be
advanced only with the greatest circumspection. Cross the minefield
we must, but hopefully without too many explosions on the way.
There are in fact two questions to be settled during the debate which
will continue throughout the present decade. Firstly, there is the
matter of the *nature* of a teacher's responsibilities; secondly, there is
the matter of their *extent*. It is easy enough to say that a teacher
should look out for the behaviour and welfare of his pupils, but how
far does that carry? To the corridor outside the classroom? To the
dinner hall? To the playground? To the gate? To the bus stop? Into
the home? Giving an answer is not difficult at the extremities but,
as Mr Banting observed, the trouble is in the middle. Most teachers
would accept responsibility for how their pupils behave in places
relatively close to the point of teaching, but distance lends not only
enchantment but also relief from a sense of obligation. Where to
draw the line is the problem in this, as in many other areas of human
activity.

Some see the solution as being the shedding of all responsibilities
beyond those narrowly confined to the communication of information in the classroom situation. Such a view was encapsulated in a

letter to *The Times* from a group of experienced teachers in the spring of 1982. They suggested that 'teachers should now reject their place "*in loco parentis*" and the whole "pastoral" rigmarole, retreating (if that is the word) to their invulnerable authority as teachers, i.e. purveyors of knowledge'. But it is precisely because of the impossibility of separating the teaching from the caring function that individual members of the profession find it difficult to decide where duty begins and ends. In the final analysis, it is unlikely that any amount of statutory or contractual provision will solve that problem. As a venerable and respected schoolmaster of my acquaintance who was much given to watching cowboy films used to say: 'A teacher's gotta do what a teacher's gotta do.'

Three

Entering the Teaching Profession

It is a truth universally acknowledged that a young person in possession of university ambitions but insufficient qualifications is likely to consider becoming a teacher. As the younger sons of the ancient nobility entered the church for lack of an inheritance, so the sixth-former without the academic credentials for a traditional university degree will very likely give at least a passing thought to entering a college of education.

But fortunately, the likelihood has declined in the present decade. It was often the case in the sixties and seventies that training to teach was seen as the logical alternative to undergraduate life when someone's A level results fell below university entrance standards. What better way to stay in the education system if one had found happiness and contentment there? One might reasonably speculate that a quarter of the practising teachers over the age of thirty are in the classroom by default. But the tide has turned in the eighties, for two reasons. Firstly, poor employment prospects give teacher training the look of a fruitless exercise. Secondly, the training institutions have moved upmarket in response to the influences at work to create an all-graduate teaching profession.

As the seventies turned the corner into the eighties, the booklet traditionally issued by the Department of Education and Science to prospective applicants for teacher training changed its tone. The November 1978 edition reflected the fact that shortage had given way to surplus: 'You may feel reluctant to apply just at the moment because of what you have heard about unemployment among teachers and, although action has been taken to reduce their

32

unemployment, it remains true that jobs cannot be guaranteed in the profession for everyone who completes training.' There followed a warning about quality: 'Although current forecasts show that there will be a need for fewer teachers in future years, it will remain an excellent career for excellent people.' Clearly, the days when young people might half-heartedly opt for teacher training as an alternative to facing the full rigours of a university course were over. The pursuit of excellence had begun. By 1980, the Department of Education and Science booklet had also changed its title, *Becoming a Teacher* giving way to *A Career in Teaching*[1]. It was fitting that a new name should be given to what was essentially a new message. Indeed, had the educational bureaucracy had the courage, the revised booklet would doubtless have been launched with a suitable slogan emblazoned across the front: *Not to be confused with the old brand of guidance.*

The new brand reflected the dramatic change which had overtaken the training institutions. During the seventies, there existed some one hundred and sixty colleges of education specialising in the training of teachers. But a major reorganisation of provision in the non-university sector led many of these colleges to merge with polytechnics, with institutions of further and higher education and with one another. Sometimes the mergers had been achieved with goodwill; sometimes colleges had been dragged kicking and screaming into unhappy alliances. A few survived as separate institutions, notably some of the most prestigious colleges run by religious denominations. But even here, the old days are gone forever and strict specialisation in teacher training is no longer the order of things.

The forces at work bringing about these changes fall into two categories: economic and educational. Since the explosion of higher education in the sixties, when an LSE lecture assumed the proportions of a Billy Graham rally, student numbers have receded. By the late seventies, many colleges of education were finding recruit-

---

1   Obtainable free of charge from the Department of Education and Science. An essential document for all prospective entrants to teacher training as it is updated annually and is probably the only absolutely reliable source of information in these changing times.

ment a serious problem. Local education authorities, who bore responsibility for a large part of the provision, were under pressure to show good stewardship and bring about rationalisation. At the same time, opinion as to the right style and content of teacher training for the eighties had been evolving in such a way to make change necessary. The prospect of entrants to the teaching profession being trained in hermetically sealed specialist institutions had diminishing appeal in a comprehensive world.

The extent to which educational philosophy adjusts itself to economic necessity is one of the true wonders of our education system. But for Cinderella's hardships, there would have been no fairy godmother to transform pumpkin into coach and white mice into dazzling ponies. Similarly, but for the barren lecture rooms in colleges of education, there might have been no such transmogrification of teacher training as we presently witness.

It would perhaps be useful at this stage to examine the alternatives now facing someone who has ambitions to become a teacher in the maintained sector of education. That is best done under three headings which themselves tell a story.

What has become almost impossible

It is now almost impossible to enter the teaching profession without a degree of some kind. The development of the Bachelor of Education (BEd) degree in the teacher training institutions, to replace the old certificate in education, has provided the basis for this. The certificate course reached its demise in 1980 and with it a route into teaching taken by some of the finest practitioners in the history of education. Whether the BEd provides all that the certificate did, and perhaps more, is discussed later in this chapter.

While the BEd is the principal means by which primary trainees now qualify, there is some evidence that secondary trainees prefer to acquire their graduate qualifications by taking traditional university degrees. The training institutions, aware of this, have attempted to match the universities by offering BA and BSc courses of various kinds. There is therefore a broad range of options available at many of them, with opportunities of transfer between them at different stages of student life. Without doubt, the institutions are better for these developments, which make past arrangements look extremely narrow and confining.

But it is not yet totally impossible to become a teacher without a degree of some kind. A new scheme of special training awards for non-graduates in craft, design and technology (CDT) will be introduced by the Department of Education and Science in September 1983, to replace one previously operated through the Manpower Services Commission[1]. There is also one other subject in which it remains worthwhile for non-graduates with an urge to teach to ask the latest situation of the Department of Education and Science, namely business studies.

The two subjects named in the previous paragraph have two things in common: there continues to be a shortage of people available to teach them and, even more important, experience outside education is of immense value in the teaching situation. There are in fact those who would argue that a mature entrant to teaching from the world of industry or business has a good deal more to offer a school than someone who comes bearing academic gifts.

What has become equally impossible

It is now almost impossible to become a teacher without taking a recognised course of professional training. The elimination of unqualified practitioners from state-school classrooms is attributable to Edward Short who, as Secretary of State for Education between 1968 and 1970, announced that people who were teaching without having been trained for the job would have to go.

To say that caused problems in the early seventies would be putting it mildly. For example, in the school of which I was headmaster at that time, it brought the business studies department to a grinding halt. The outstanding but unqualified head of department was quite prepared to go and train as a teacher, but her

---

1 Details are contained in a booklet entitled *Teacher Training Awards in Craft, Design and Technology*, obtainable from the Department of Education and Science.

scant academic credentials denied her a college place. As a result, she was forced to abandon teaching, leaving behind not a few colleagues whose professional competence, on their own admission, fell well below hers. Schools still talk about the losses they sustained when Edward Short swept away unqualified teachers, but he was right to do it. Any significant social change encompasses a few disadvantages in its overall achievements, but if teaching is ever completely to become a profession, there can be no place in its ranks for people who are not qualified to practise. The fact that some can prove themselves quite good at it by picking it up as they go along is neither here nor there. There have been cases of people posing as surgeons and successfully carrying out operations. Few would argue that, on being caught, they should continue practising on grounds of having somehow acquired the knack of carving people up without killing them.

But it remains possible for someone to become a teacher without meeting the training requirement if he or she is a mathematician or scientist, although that will not apply to any significant extent for much longer. Change was presaged in the autumn 1982 edition of *A Career in Teaching* in a specific reference to people with mathematical and scientific qualifications and an urge to enter the world of pedagogy: 'At present these are exempt from the requirement because of the shortage in these subjects, but this exemption may be reviewed, and many teachers elect to take the training course.' At the beginning of 1983, the Advisory Committee on the Supply and Training of Teachers (ACSET) made a recommendation to the Secretary of State that mathematics and science graduates should no longer be exempt from teacher training requirements. By way of a response, Sir Keith Joseph indicated his intention to withdraw blanket exemption at the end of 1983. However, he will still 'stand ready to consider recognising as qualified teachers untrained graduates in mathematics and science, in individual cases and on supply grounds on the recommendation of local education authorities. He judges that this will be a sufficient protection for supply in present circumstances.' (White Paper *Teaching Quality,* March 1983) Thus does the creation of a properly trained profession wait upon the emergence of a sufficient supply of teachers in shortage subjects.

Which being so, almost any attempt to increase the number of mathematics, physics and chemistry graduates entering the profession is worth a try. But even as these words are being written, rumour has it that the Secretary of State's recently-launched pilot scheme for awarding tax-free scholarships of £500 to selected graduates in the subjects named who undertake teacher training, and guaranteeing them posts afterwards, is doomed to failure.[1]

Degrees of difference

Leaving aside special schemes devised to deal with exceptional shortages, there are three ways in which a potential teacher may acquire the graduate status and professional training now necessary for admission as a classroom practitioner:

by taking a three-year course leading to an ordinary BEd degree or a four-year course leading to an honours BEd degree;

by taking a degree other than a BEd, followed by a one-year course for the Postgraduate Certificate in Education (PGCE);

by taking a four-year course which incorporates teacher training in a degree other than a BEd.

Someone might follow the first route by going to a college of education or one of the institutes of higher education formed in the way described earlier in this chapter. The second alternative might also be available there, but someone following this route into teaching would perhaps be more likely to take his or her degree at a university before looking round for the best place to study for the PGCE. The third alternative is only available in a few places, mostly universities, and tends to relate to certain specialisms. For example, someone wishing to teach the deaf might seek a place in the department of audiology at Manchester University where the honours degree awarded after four years of study embraces a teaching qualification.

1 Abandonment of the scheme has since been announced on the grounds that graduates coming forward were not of a sufficiently high calibre. The conclusions to be drawn are various.

The difference between one degree and another is of no small interest to the teaching profession, and the emergence of the BEd in the seventies had a distracting effect upon the bridge players to be found in the staffrooms of the best quality comprehensives, which had not so long before been grammar schools. A further decline in standards was clearly threatened by the establishment of a degree that was so obviously not a degree. 'What on earth is the point', asked one whose contracts at cards were more often completed than his marking, 'of pretending that something with a daft name like BEd will turn this into a graduate profession? B silly I call it.'

But, despite unpromising predictions, the BEd has taken a firm hold and appears to be flourishing. A report published at the end of 1980 showed that forty-four BEd programmes had been validated by the Council for National Academic Awards (CNAA), the body responsible for setting and monitoring the standards for the majority of such courses. But the report, entitled *School Experience in Initial BEd and BEd Honours Courses Validated by the CNAA,* sounded some warnings. Courses were overcrowded with aims and objectives, and failed to establish the relationship between theory and practice. One passage summed up the problem:

> If students are to be asked to integrate the philosophical, psychological and sociological theories of education they are introduced to, and reflect this integration in their practice of teaching, then college staff ought firstly to be aware of what they are asking, secondly be able to do it themselves and finally be able to show students how to do it.

As a solution, the report proposed that ordinary BEd courses should be extended from three to four years. For the first two years, students would spend their time in mixed interest groups working towards the Diploma in Higher Education (Dip HE). Professional studies would be concentrated almost entirely in the third and fourth years.

It is already possible in some institutes to spend two years studying for a Dip HE and then transfer to the third year of a BEd, and the CNAA proposal would simply mean the extension of this principle more widely. One argument in favour is that it would allow students to delay their commitment to teaching, since the Dip HE is a qualification in its own right.

But the commonest complaint of student teachers is that they have to wait too long before getting into the classroom. Under existing arrangements, someone keen to get on with it and discover what it is really like at the chalkface will often have to wait until the fifth term of training before spending any significant amount of time in a school. There is an important issue at stake here. Most qualified teachers give the same reply to the question: 'What was the most valuable part of your training?' The answer almost every time comes in two words: 'Teaching practice.' Would it not be best if those considering teaching as a career got the feel of it *before* committing themselves to a lengthy training course? No, I am not talking about sixth-formers being allowed to have a go with the slow learners in their schools or being sent off, in what are euphemistically known as private study periods, to see what really goes on in the local primaries. What some argue for, myself among them, is a thorough-going experience of a school for one full term before commencing training; in short, a return to the pupil–teacher concept. This blatantly reactionary proposal would solve one of the most serious problems facing the training institutions. Having accepted students and consumed several years of their lives in preparing them as teachers, tutors find it almost impossible to recommend failure. Some attribute this to moral sensitivity; others to lack of moral fibre. My own experience as a CNAA teaching-practice examiner suggests that the first is closer to the truth than the second.

But two other factors are also at work. On asking one tutor how it was that a particularly unsuitable student had been allowed to stay on the course, I was told: 'There would be hell to pay with the student body if we started failing people. We depend on you to do that for us.' Unhappily, the second of the other factors is no more noble than the first. When the education wing of an institute of higher education is fighting for its survival, student recruitment becomes critical in terms of numbers rather than quality.

My own teacher training began in the classroom. Correction; it began in the headmaster's study. Before being launched upon a group of unsuspecting seven-year-olds, I was advised: 'Be a beast.

But a just beast.' For a starter, fresh up to college from home a few days before, it was sound advice. The ensuing days were the most terrifying, exhausting and exhilarating of my life up to that point. By the end of the practice, I was on the way to discovering the truth that all must find who think to make teaching in the maintained sector a career. It is unarguably, indisputably, incontrovertibly the case that one must positively enjoy being in the company of young people of all sorts and conditions.

Nothing that subsequently happened to me in a teaching career covering twenty-three years altered my opinion about that priority. More important for the present discussion, there was no other way of discovering it than by coming eyeball to eyeball in the classroom with those on the receiving end of education. The longer that moment is postponed in teacher training, the worse it is and will continue to be for the profession.

Seeing how unattractive some teachers find children to be, it is a mystery how they came to enter a profession that compels them to spend so much time in their company. Rarely a week went by without Mr Robbins storming out of his music classes into the staffroom to announce, with a slam of the door and a crash of books on the table: 'I hate them. I *hate* them!' That, believe it or not, was in a grammar school. Dare one speculate upon what Mr Robbins has to say about his pupils now that comprehensivisation has come upon him? There is no more sad spectacle in the teaching profession than he or she made bitter by dislike of children.

Since training to teach by the BEd method is the most common, it is disturbing that current practice and proposals for the future seem to favour postponing the moment when would-be teachers begin to find out whether or not they are actually going to enjoy spending five days a week for forty years with groups of children made up of polite ones and rude ones; shining ones and dirty smelly ones; kind ones and bullies; clever ones and ones for whom school will forever be a steeplechase where every fence is Becher's Brook.

It is not beyond the bounds of possibility that some potentially outstanding teachers have been discouraged from entering into training because of the amount of time and attention courses devote to matters other than practical teaching. James Galway, the eminent flute-player, has some opinions on the training of musicians which are relevant. When he was interviewed on BBC radio in 1982, he was asked why he had never attended the Royal College of Music or any similar training institution. His answer was that such places did not allow a musician actually to get on with playing an instrument, which was all he had ever wished to do. Masses of time was spent on musical theory and everyone had to take singing lessons. It was, James Galway insisted, like someone wanting to run a four-minute mile being made to study anatomy and physiology for a couple of years before being allowed to set foot on the running track. It is to be profoundly hoped that, as the BEd continues to develop in the mid-eighties and beyond, pressure to postpone classroom experience in order to provide multi-purpose courses will be resisted.

Whether someone enters teaching by the BEd route or some other, there is a new requirement applicable from 1984 onwards that deserves mention at this point. All who complete their training in that year must have a pass at O level in English and mathematics to qualify to teach. It is a provision long overdue. In George Orwell's *Nineteen Eighty Four,* Big Brother's henchmen went to a great deal of trouble to reduce Winston Smith to a condition where he got his sums wrong. With far less effort, our education system has created the same condition in a great many children. It is astonishing that evidence of numeracy and literacy has not pre-viously been required for entry to the teaching profession. There is a certain dramatic significance in the fact that the year 1984 will see that put right.

If Her Majesty's Inspectors are to be believed, that will still leave a great deal to be done about the competence of those entering teaching. In October 1982, they published a report entitled *The New Teacher in School* which constituted a devastating attack upon the condition of the profession. About a quarter of newly qualified teachers were alleged to lack the skills necessary to be effective in the classroom. *The Times* published two letters on the report. The first came from Max Morris, than whom there has never been a more persistent advocate of improved standards within the profession. The second was my response to his observations. Extracts from both letters, taken together, serve to highlight the aspects of teacher training which cause experienced professionals concern.

Max Morris

That a certain number of the newly qualified are 'lacking in the skills they need for the job' has for a long time been a matter of common observation. I have not been alone over the years in suggesting the need for a thorough enquiry into both the *content* of teacher training and the practical experience in schools of the trainers.

It is, for example, worth examining whether the major reorganisation of secondary education on comprehensive lines has been matched in the colleges and university departments by the appointment of staff thoroughly experienced in the new system and the teaching problems associated with an unselective pupil entry. Have education departments in the training institutions been able to teach from practical experience about the curricular problems involved? Is the kind of educational sociology, now an integral part of training, being taught designed to be helpful to the teacher in the classroom or is it airy-fairy theorising? These are just a few of the worrying questions that arise from the Inspectorate's report.

Peter Dawson

True, the content of teacher training needs to be reconsidered, along with the ability of the present generation of teacher trainers to carry out the task laid upon them.

But the really important question is not how teachers are trained but how they are selected.

There is little doubt that a good many of the young teachers condemned by Her Majesty's Inspectors in the report to which Mr Morris refers should never have been admitted to the profession in the first place.

Colleges are, in my experience, extremely reluctant to fail student teachers once they have been selected for training. Similarly, local authority advisers and inspectors are disinclined to fail probationers outright after they have completed a long period of training. In short, once a sixth-former has been accepted for training as a teacher, only an utterly disastrous performance over a period of several years will prevent him or her from becoming a fully qualified teacher with a secure place within the profession.

The story would, of course, be very different if the profession itself set the standards for admission. The establishment of a General Teaching Council with appropriate powers would bring about a major improvement in the quality of teachers in this country in a very short time.

There now exists an organisation dedicated to giving teachers a proper professional voice in their own affairs. A leading member of the Campaign for the General Teaching Council (CATEC) has provided an appendix to this book, describing the structure and powers a GTC might have. At the annual conference of the NUT at Easter 1983, the General Secretary added his voice to those calling for the establishment of a professional body for teachers. But while we await its formation – and the wait is likely to be a long one – other developments indicate that the second half of the eighties will witness the proper involvement of the teaching profession in the education of educators.

In January 1983 there appeared *Teaching in Schools: The Content of Initial Training,* the Inspectorate's sequel to their report on new teachers. Its observations were breathtaking in their simplicity. 'Selection of the right students', it was proclaimed, 'is the first step in providing the right kind of teachers.' Teacher training should be carried out 'by people who are successful and experienced members of the teaching profession, up-to-date in their knowledge of schools'. Practising teachers and teacher trainers should teach in each others institutions.

In the spring of 1983, these propositions gathered momentum when they appeared in the White Paper *Teaching Quality* – a document which will almost certainly reshape teacher training in the next ten years. Its principal provisions are six:

1   Approval of teacher training courses will in future depend upon their conformity to specific criteria. Promulgation of these by the Secretary of State for Education and Science and the Secretary of State for Wales will be carried out in consultation with the Advisory Committee on the Supply

and Education of Teachers (ACSET). Once the criteria are formulated and published, 'the Secretaries of State will initiate a review of all existing approved courses of initial training. They may withdraw approval from those courses which do not conform to the criteria.'[1]

2   The criteria will impose three broad requirements upon all courses of training, namely that academic standards are high enough to give teachers what is called 'subject expertise', that there is adequate attention to teaching method 'differentiated by age of intended pupils', and that there is a close link between theory and practice 'involving the active participation of experienced practising school teachers'.

3   With regard to the third of the broad requirements, the establishment of close links between schools and training institutions at a local level is seen as essential. It is necessary that 'a sufficient proportion of each institution's staff should have enjoyed success as teachers in school, and their school experience should be recent, substantial and relevant'. To that end, joint teacher/tutor appointments are recommended and schemes of teacher/tutor exchange.

4   The selection of students for training needs in future to be carried out with greater care, with practising teachers being involved in the process.

5   Institutions must be less reluctant in future to fail students whose classroom performance is suspect. 'The Secretaries of State', it is asserted, 'will expect institutions not to award to a student whose practical classroom work is not satisfactory a BEd degree or PGCE which entitles him to recognition as a qualified teacher.'

6   Recognised teacher status will in future carry with it an element of specificity. A course of training will only be approved under the new criteria if it prepares teachers 'to work with pupils within a specific age range, and in the

1   ACSET has moved with astonishing speed, submitting its advice to the Secretaries of State in August 1983. Details are provided in the fourth appendix to this book.

case of secondary courses to teach specific subjects'. In future, letters issued by the Secretary of State notifying trainees that they have qualified 'will specifically draw attention to the phase and subjects for which the course of initial training was intended'. In order to ensure that newcomers to the profession are only appointed to posts whose requirements match their specific qualifications, the Secretary of State will amend the *Education (Teachers) Regulations 1982* 'so as to require employers to have regard to the formal qualifications of teachers in determining whether or not the staff of teachers in any school is suitable'.

It is the last of these measures which undoubtedly presents the greatest threat to the freedom of the teaching profession from central control. If implemented to any significant degree, it will mean that head teachers are no longer able to make their own judgements as to whom it would be best to appoint to any particular post in given circumstances. The White Paper comes dangerously close to making a fool of itself in its references to the mismatch between some teachers' qualifications and the subjects they are teaching. What subjects are mentioned as examples? The citing of mathematics and physics gives the game away. With the acute shortage of properly qualified and trained teachers in these disciplines that has obtained for as long as anyone can remember, the head teacher has had to persuade whomsoever he can to teach them in order to make a timetable. When there are few fish to be had, he must be prepared to net just about anything that comes swimming in the direction of his educational trawler. It is no good a starving man demanding fat mackerel when there are only sprats in the sea. If there is in future to be a closer identification of qualifications and teaching commitments in those areas of the curriculum where the greatest mismatch at present applies, something dramatic has to be done about recruitment. How are more people of the right quality to be persuaded to apply for teacher training? On that subject, *Teaching Quality* is strangely silent.

A further development at the beginning of 1983 is also destined to have an important influence on the future condition of the teaching profession, namely measures to improve provision for probationer teachers. What sort of teacher an individual becomes depends to a great extent on his or her experience during the first year in the classroom. There was a time when a newcomer to the staff of a school was given the most difficult classes as a matter of course. One of the rewards of long service in the secondary sector was a gradual progression across the territory of the timetable from the rugged terrain of the most disruptive fourth-formers to the fertile plains of the brightest eleven-year-olds. In the heyday of the maintained grammar school, the location of staff on Friday afternoons told an interesting story. At that most difficult of times for teaching children, it was the experienced practitioners who were to be found supping tea and reading the newspapers in the staffroom while the youngsters were sent forth to handle the heavy brigade. This was justified on two grounds. Firstly, it was conveniently believed that throwing new teachers in at the deep end was the best way of helping them to learn the trade. Secondly, it was held to be a self-evident truth that one of the rights which went with promotion was an easier life.

There are still a few schools in which the old military principle applies that raw recruits must expect to be used as cannon fodder while the officer corps distances itself from the fray. But the treatment of young teachers has of necessity improved with the arrival of the large comprehensive school. The reason is not hard to discern. While it was one thing to use the sink-or-swim approach in relatively small establishments containing pupils of similar ability and disposition, it is quite another to expect a new teacher to survive without considerable support in a comprehensive crystal palace. If the comprehensive has done nothing else, it has focussed attention on the need for young teachers to be carefully nurtured. Another factor making that necessary has been the development at all ages and levels of ability within the school system of greater freedom for pupils. The maintenance of good discipline is today considerably more difficult than it was when every child in a primary school class was doing more or less the same thing at the same time.

Schedule 6 of the *Education (Teachers) Regulations 1982* requires local education authorities to ensure that a probationer is provided with such conditions of work and supervision as to ensure 'a fair and effective assessment of his conduct and efficiency as a teacher'. By way of guidance to local education authorities on how to set about meeting the requirements of Schedule 6, the Department of Education and Science issued an administrative memorandum in January 1983 entitled *The Treatment and Assessment of Probationary Teachers*. Its principal elements will without doubt transform provision for young teachers as the eighties unfold:

3a   All new teachers required to serve a period of probation to be informed in writing of the period they have to serve.

4a   Care to be taken in making appointments 'to ensure that there is prospect of continuous service for the requisite probation period. The duties assigned to a probationer, supervision and conditions of work should be such as to facilitate a fair and reasonable assessment of conduct and efficiency as a teacher'.

4c   Probationers to be given an opportunity 'to demonstrate their proficiency in teaching classes of a size normal for the school in which they teach, and the subject they are teaching'.

5   Probationers to be placed in posts 'closely related to the age groups and subjects for which they have been trained'. Probationers should not be appointed to schools 'which present unusual problems of discipline or teaching techniques unless they have been trained to meet such problems, or can be given special support to help cope with them'.

6a   Comparable and equitable arrangements for the assessment of probationers to be provided by a local education authority in all its schools.

6b   The following opportunities to be made available to a probationer before an appointment is taken up:
   (i)   a visit to the school to meet the headteacher, the head of department where appropriate and fellow members of staff;

(ii) information from the school in the form of a school handbook or similar document giving useful facts about organisation;

(iii) adequate notice of the timetable to be taught;

(iv) all necessary syllabuses or schemes of work within which the probationer will be operating;

(v) information about equipment and other resources available for use;

(vi) information about support and supervision provided by the local education authority.

6c Probationers to be given the following opportunities after taking up appointment:

(i) to be able to seek help and guidance from a nominated member of staff and the head of department, as appropriate;

(ii) to be able to observe lessons given by experienced colleagues;

(iii) to visit other appropriate schools;

(iv) to have some lessons observed and assessed by colleagues and local education authority advisers, and receive advice as a result;

(v) to be able to have discussions with other probationers;

(vi) to attend any meeting of probationers organised by the local education authority.

6d Probationers to be made aware of 'the criteria on which they will be assessed'. These criteria to include 'class management, relevant subject expertise, appropriate teaching skills, adequacy of lesson preparation, use of resources, understanding the needs of pupils, ability to establish appropriate relationships with pupils and colleagues'.

7a Probationers to be made aware at the outset of the methods of assessment to be used and the people responsible for the assessment.

7b Probationers to have the opportunity to discuss their progress with those responsible for assessing them 'in time for them to heed advice before an assessment is made'.

7c Probationers to be informed at an early stage when problems make an adverse assessment likely, 'be warned of the consequences and be given an opportunity to heed advice'.

8 A probationer who fails to make satisfactory progress in one school to be moved to another school, perhaps with an extension of probation. The initiative for a change 'might come from the probationer's assessors or from the probationer'.

9b When a decision to extend probation is likely, the probationer to be given 'an opportunity to make representations, including oral representations, accompanied by a friend, immediately before any such decision is made'.

9c Where a local education authority decides to recommend to the Secretary of State that a probationer be declared unsuitable, Her Majesty's Inspector to be informed 'in sufficient time for him to arrange to visit the probationer in order to make an independent assessment'.

Since the *Education (Teachers) Regulations 1982* constitute a statutory instrument, every local education authority is bound to devise some kind of code of provision for probationers and it is likely that the guidance provided by the Department of Education and Science will be closely observed. That is made all the more likely by a footnote to the administrative memorandum (the italics are mine):

In considering any appeal against dismissal by a failed probationer, industrial tribunals have no power to question the professional judgement of a probationer's competence, properly and reasonably exercised, but they do take great pains to discover whether a probationary teacher has been fairly treated during probation, particularly in regard to the support given, the conditions in which the probation has been served, e.g. the

suitability of the post(s) occupied, and whether the probationer has had adequate advice and warning on performance.
A structured plan for the support and supervision of probationary
teachers should therefore be devised by each local education authority.

Adequate provision for probationers begins with their being
clearly identified. Lest that be thought a statement of the monumen-
tally obvious and therefore totally unnecessary, the case of the Inner
London Education Authority *versus* Lloyd in the Court of Appeal in
the spring of 1981 indicates why attention needs to be drawn to the
matter. To cut a very long legal story short, the ILEA dismissed Mr
Lloyd from his post at Kingsdale School in Dulwich for incompetence after having overlooked the fact that he was a probationer. An
industrial tribunal found that the dismissal was unfair and this was
supported by Lord Justice Eveleigh, Lord Justice Watkins and Sir
David Cairns in the Court of Appeal in the following terms:

> The industrial tribunal were entitled to find that the respon-
> dent employee had been unfairly dismissed, notwithstanding
> that he was not capable of properly performing his work, in
> circumstances where the appellant employers had not realised
> that he was a probationary teacher until seventeen months into
> his two-year probationary period. The industrial tribunal had
> not acted perversely in taking the view that as a probationer
> the respondent was entitled to appropriate advice and guidance
> and that the employers acted unreasonably in treating his
> incompetence as a sufficient reason for dismissing, since over
> the whole period he did not get the same help that he would
> have got in the ordinary course of events had it been known
> that he was a probationer right from the beginning.

The day of adequate support and consideration for probationers
has arrived. That is fine, provided it does not deny children the
support and protection they deserve to have from poor teachers.
Does one detect in the code of guidance just a suggestion that
someone who should never have been allowed to train as a teacher in
the first place is to be advised, protected, counselled, allowed to
appeal against unfavourable assessments, moved from school to

school, given a further period of probation and permitted to stay in the classroom at almost any cost to those the profession exists to serve? May it not prove to be so.

The majority of probationers do not have any great difficulty in settling happily to the art and science of teaching, so I will not dwell longer on the difficulties faced by some. Allow me instead to bring this chapter to a close by referring to those who are destined to become good teachers and who take to the classroom like Long John Silver to a tot of rum. There seem to me three skills that a teacher needs to develop as quickly as possible. The first has to do with organisation, the second with discipline and the third with humour.

Organisation

Mr Bradley, a linguist, started every term with a new mark book and a determination to keep a proper record of his pupils' work. He would declare his good intentions to the whole staffroom, like someone coming forward at an evangelical rally to give himself to a new way of life. But it never lasted. First his marking would get behind, then his recording of it, until he gave up any serious attempt to cope with either about half way through the term. When there were examination papers to cope with as well, panic replaced lethargy. Mr Wingate, a convert to geography from PE as the years took their toll of wind and sinew, offered his personal remedy for the examination paper problem: 'Try stair marking.' A young probationer myself, the concept was new to me, so I listened intently to the explanation. 'Take a set of exam papers. Go to the top of the stairs at home, and throw 'em down. The one that lands on the top stair gets top mark, and so on all the way down to the one that lands in the hall.' Somewhat unnecessarily, Mr Wingate added: 'It saves a lot of time.'

Marking is like the washing and ironing: it just keeps coming round. Unless a teacher comes to terms with it early on by getting properly organised, it can become something of a nightmare trying to keep up with it. Marking and returning exercises punctiliously makes a world of difference to one's relationship with a class and one's ability to build from lesson to lesson upon material presented.

Mathematicians know this well and are usually good markers. Theirs is manifestly a sequential subject in which a proper grasp of one concept is essential before moving on to another. But many subjects are not of that kind and it is possible to leave work on one topic unmarked while starting up the study of another. It is a temptation the young teacher should resist at all costs.

Another area in which it is essential to get organised early on is that of lesson preparation. Unlike marking, this problem tends to diminish over the years, although the notion that, once you have got through a full academic year, you are set up with teaching notes for the next forty is not to be encouraged. That attitude is encapsulated in the story of the old-timer who, to mark the Queen's Silver Jubilee in 1977, decided to use the teaching notes he had prepared when she came to the throne. On investigation, he discovered that he was in fact already doing so.

It is hard to generalise about exactly how a young teacher should set about making preparation and marking part of his or her lifestyle. But simply recognising that it has to be done is an important victory, as when a householder comes to accept that gardening, like it or not, is part of the package in a property-owning democracy. In short, there is no way of becoming an effective teacher except by acknowledging from the start that a good deal of one's private time has to be taken up with preparing teaching materials and correcting children's work. Professionalism demands a high level of commitment to these things.

Mrs Lockyer applied her own particular sanctions on occasions when salary negotiations failed to deliver the goods she had ordered: she would simply decline to do anything connected with school outside the strict limits of her teaching timetable. Her tactics were the logical extension of attitudes described elsewhere in this book in connection with definition of a teacher's duties. They represent a massive departure from genuine professionalism. It is in fact impossible to confine one's obligations to anything so narrow as a school timetable. Teaching is not so much a programme, more a way of life.

Discipline

PGCE students in the education department at Southampton University are given some unambiguous advice in preparation for their first teaching practice: 'Don't smile for a week.' It reflects the fear which is in the heart of every fledgling teacher – that of losing control in the classroom. There is not a shadow of doubt that discipline is the first and greatest worry of every new practitioner, not to mention a goodly number who have been at the chalkface for years. Unless one establishes effective disciplinary techniques in the early years, decades of misery stretch ahead. I use the term *disciplinary techniques* deliberately, to emphasise my view that effective classroom control is not just a matter of flair and personality. To listen to some pundits, one would think the only people who should be encouraged to enter teaching are those who subtly combine the natural authority of Mahatma Gandhi with the self-confidence of Muhammad Ali and the wit of Oscar Wilde. While it is true that ability to relate to children and young people is important and that it cannot be acquired if one happens to have no trace of it, there are certain techniques which will help the average recruit to teaching develop whatever natural resources he or she possesses.

In the mid-seventies, the senior members of staff of the school at which I was at the time headmaster drew up a list of ten techniques or practical hints for maintaining order in the classroom. They were listed in my earlier book *Making a Comprehensive Work*. Judging by the interest shown in them since, it is worthwhile reproducing them here. In places they are, of course, expressed in terms particular to one school's style of organisation, but the general principles remain clear. It is perhaps worth adding that they come from a group of professionals with literally hundreds of years experience in the classroom between them.

1   *Start right.* Train your classes to line up outside classrooms and enter them in an orderly way.

2   *Go properly equipped.* Make sure you have with you everything you need for the lesson you have prepared. Do

not send children on errands to fetch things: if you are disorganised your class will catch the same spirit.

3   *Be equipped for the worst.* It's a good idea always to have with you a box of pencils and a packet of paper for children who have come without their equipment, otherwise you may spend the first half of a lesson organising loans between pupils. But leave five minutes at the end to get your property back.

4   *Keep a register of each class,* and mark it before the lesson begins, so that you know exactly who is there, and so that the children know that you know.

5   *Reduce behaviour problems to individuals.* Most unruly classes are like that because of one or two individuals. Mass punishments are usually ineffective. Thirty children do not mind being kept in together: there is a *camaraderie* of affliction in that situation. Hence, class detentions are not permitted. The important thing is to isolate individuals. Here are some ways of doing that:

   (a)   Separate your problem pupil within the classroom: put him at the front on his own and give him a special task to get on with while you teach the rest.

   (b)   Put your problem pupil outside in the corridor. But first make sure there is no one outside the door of another classroom in the same corridor: two villains in the corridor together spell trouble.

   (c)   Ask a senior colleague next door or nearby to take your problem pupil into his or her class.

6   *Only threaten once,* then carry out your threat to the letter. For example, if you have said you will put a boy outside if he fools about again, do it the moment he repeats his offence. Never threaten what you cannot or do not intend to carry out. Never make repeated threats. Some experienced teachers would say never threaten at all, just go ahead and punish the first time a pupil offends. There is nothing wrong with that advice.

7   *Set extra work.* This is an effective sanction in the case of relatively able and well-behaved pupils whose behaviour

has lapsed. It's no good for pupils of little ability or those who never get their work in on time anyway. You will end up by making work for yourself if you set additional assignments for boys and girls who will have to be chased for weeks afterwards to deliver the goods. If you do set extra work, it must be in your own subject: it is unprofessional to use someone else's subject as a punishment. The setting of lines is not permitted.

8   *Call in senior staff* if you have persistent problems. We have *all* had discipline problems in our careers and there is nothing to be ashamed about if you have them. It's better to ask for help too soon than too late. Take particular note of the following:

(a)   Your head of department is responsible for discipline within your department, so make sure he or she knows your problems.

(b)   Also make sure a pupil's head of year is informed if there is serious and/or persistent trouble. Other departments may be complaining about the same pupil you are struggling with, in which case a red card will be issued. These two points are very important. If you isolate yourself with your problems they will overwhelm you. Heads of departments and heads of years expect to be told what is going on: they are answerable if you have a disaster. Put notes in their pigeon-holes if you aren't going to see them soon after any disciplinary event.

9   *In an emergency, stop everything.* What troubles most young teachers is the question of what to do when a pupil (or sometimes a whole class) gets out of hand. If that happens, do one of these things:

(a)   Ask your colleague next door to watch your class while you bring the offending pupil to the office wing to be dealt with. If the pupil can be relied on to report to the office wing without escort, send him down on his own. But if you do this, check afterwards that he got there.

(b) If a whole class becomes unmanageable, go and fetch the nearest senior member of staff (your head of department is first choice if nearby). Before getting to situation (b), you might try stopping your carefully prepared lesson and making the whole class get their heads down to some writing (another reason for always having spare paper and pencils with you: see item 3 above).

10 *Good discipline is not a matter of tricks.* It is a matter of proper professional attention to the job in hand and an unremitting effort to master the art and science of teaching. Good discipline arises from self-discipline and it begins with the teacher: we must be disciplined ourselves if we are to get the behaviour we want from children. That means being on time, being prepared for whatever may happen, and insisting on good standards. Here is how to get good discipline: be punctual, be prepared and be persistent.

Discipline is one of life's paradoxes, in that it leads not to repression but freedom. The teacher who has no discipline dare not allow children to wander about the classroom at will, because chaos will ensue. Conversely, the teacher who has control over what goes on may allow a great deal of liberty, secure in the knowledge that, when the children are told to return to their desks, sit up and listen, they will do so. It is those who lack discipline who are repressive, not those who possess it. They shout and rave and threaten and treat alike large misdemeanours and small. Fifteen-year-old Sally Jackson was sent to my study for not putting the date at the top of her work. Challenged later about this case of overkill, her teacher explained: 'I told them and told them the next one to give any trouble would be sent to you, and it just happened to be her.' Prior to Sally's massive misdemeanour, two boys had drawn blood from one another in a scuffle, one chair had been broken and the blackboard duster had been thrown out of the window. Sally the can-carrier was not oblivious to the injustice done to her as a result of her teacher's incompetence. Schools where discipline is generally poor are full of unfairness.

Young people much prefer a structured environment where someone is clearly in control to one where disobedience and disorder hold sway. A class quickly tires of being allowed to do as it likes. The most popular teachers, as well as the most successful ones, are those who have a grip on things. The foolish notion that discipline is in some way objectionable has led some teachers astray. It is well to remember that the first thing the Bible tells us about God is that he made pronouncements that brought order out of chaos and the first thing it tells us about Jesus as a teacher is that he taught with authority.

Humour

The exercise of authority does not require a teacher constantly to present a face that looks like one of those steel-bound executive briefcases. Thus, while it may indeed be wise not to smile for the first week with a new class, that is but the beginning. Learning to relax and employ a touch of humour is a critical skill for a teacher to develop. As we grow in our relationships with those we teach, there must come a revealing of our true selves if the right kind of communication is to be established.

His Honour Judge Brian Galpin tells how he received a new driving licence in which he was described as His Brian Galpin. He comments: 'I now drive secure in the knowledge that I nothing lack if I am His.' The moral of this story is that mistakes made by others sometimes bring reassurance. It is one which has a particular application in schools.

Some newcomers to the profession believe they have always to preserve an image of stern infallibility before children. That way lies certain disaster, since the simple business of writing in a straight line across a blackboard takes most of us some time to master. One's spelling is also inclined to fall apart when the chalk is in the hand and many a young teacher's confidence has been shattered on having his weakness in that department pointed out by thirty cockahoop youngsters, all pointing to the blackboard at once. The standard tactic of declaring you did it on purpose to see who was paying attention is only effective if delivered in such a way as to make it clear that you are not being serious. To repeat, stern infallibility is not the way. Taking oneself none too seriously is a most effective way of establishing rapport with the young, who generally find life amusing anyway, not yet having embarked upon the grim struggle to earn a living, pay the mortgage and buy their own toothpaste.

An entrant to teaching also needs a sense of humour to survive the company of colleagues. Not a few quite passable classroom practitioners have come to grief over relationships which revolve around the staffroom tea urn, the profession being a collection of extraordinary types. But that is a story for another chapter of this book.

Entering the teaching profession has become a very different enterprise from that of a few years ago and will continue to change further as the eighties unfold. Selection and training, and the institutions in which training takes place, have been transformed of late and the process of transformation continues. Out of all this higher professional standards will hopefully come.

But the essential basis upon which good teaching depends will not change. If there is one point in the preceding pages that needs emphasising above all else it is that prospective entrants to the profession should only step over the threshold if they have genuine liking for the company of the young. Liking one's subject is not enough; liking the teaching process is not enough; liking one's own experience of school as a pupil is not enough. Only a quite profound affection for the up-and-coming generation with all its wonders and its horrors will do. John Colet knew the truth of it: 'Teach what thou has learned *lovingly*.' Once more, the italics are mine.

Four

Pupil Participation

In his book *The Queen's Government,* Sir Ivor Jennings asserted that the ordinary Englishman was not only a free man, but truculently free. Furthermore, his was a freedom both of movement and of thought. But a note of reservation was added:

> Even now the education which we give to the mass of our citizens is so inferior that they cannot make adequate use of the knowledge open to them. Freedom of thought is therefore not a particularly valuable principle to them, for they have not learned to think.

Those words were written not at some point in the distant past, before Miss Buss and Miss Beale entered the barren educational scene. The first edition of Jennings' book appeared in January 1953, the year our present monarch was crowned.

Thirty years later, it would be argued by some that Jennings' strictures on the education system no longer apply. But, interestingly enough, the Minister of the Queen's Government with responsibility for education would not agree. In 1982, the Secretary of State for Education and Science suggested in more than one quarter that children in school stood in need of being taught to reason. Sir Keith Joseph raised the issue with me in a private meeting in October of that year and was clearly of the view that the forward march of the state education system had failed to provide the great majority of young people with the ability to think rationally.

Now if it be true that, for all that has been done since 1944 and before that to establish an effective education system in this country, the products of our schools are not being encouraged to develop the

power to reason, that is a serious matter. It is so because Sir Ivor
Jennings was undoubtedly right: those who have not learned to
think for themselves about the information that is offered to them
cannot be truly free. Despite Cowper's observation that when
reasoning at every step man yet mistakes the way, there is a duty
upon teachers to engender in their pupils the capacity to weigh up
what they see and hear and experience in a rational manner and then,
fearlessly and with malice toward none, draw their own conclusions.
But for most of its history, the education system has not encouraged
the development of critical faculties in children. As a result, those
who teach sixth-formers almost invariably have difficulty in encouraging them to question the pronouncements of this or that
authority on a subject. University tutors constantly complain that
schools do not train young people to arrive at their own judgements.
A Cambridge don summed up one group of prospective under-
graduates at the end of a day of interviews: 'They had all read the
right books, but only one of them had any ideas of his own.' That is
a judgement on the teaching profession and the origins of the
problem need to be examined.

It is first necessary to acknowledge that making judgements for
oneself is a mature activity which only becomes possible after one
has accumulated a good deal of knowledge and had a significant
range of experiences. It is not possible to teach a primary school
child to examine and question the evidence for this or that
interpretation of what happened at Agincourt or Austerlitz. One
teaches certain facts, some of which may only be someone's opinion,
and waits for a later day to raise the complex issue of historicity. The
same principle applies in the life of a school outside the curriculum.
Firstly, rules of behaviour are taught and perhaps the need for them
explained. Only later, when those subject to them have acquired a
degree of maturity, is it possible to have a comprehensive discussion
on their validity. Indeed, with regard both to curricular and
behavioural matters, small children are likely to become confused if
asked to make their own judgements as to what to accept.

So much is fairly obvious. The problem lies in deciding when the
time has come for school pupils to be taught to question and
challenge what one is offering to them. The polar extremes are not

hard to identify. At five the exercise is premature; at eighteen it is too late. The difficulty, as Odysseus discovered in attempting to pass both the monster and the whirlpool, is in finding the right point in between. It might seem reasonable to assume that the time to develop the critical faculties of the young is in the middle years of secondary education. By then they are equipped to make judgements and, equally to the point, keen to do so. If motivation is the key to successful education, which it undoubtedly is, there is surely no better moment to give a youngster his or her critical head than as thirteen years are left behind and the fourteenth gets under way. But at precisely that point the Scylla of public examinations emerges from its cave and drags them in. Given the extent of the material to be taught in most subjects, covering the syllabus becomes the chief preoccupation of teachers, rather than encouraging pupils to think critically about the information being offered to them. It is a sad truth that it is quite possible to do well at O level by purchasing one of those little crammers that are available in bookshops.

It is remarkable that the deliverance of schools from the grip of constricting public examination syllabuses is being achieved through the Certificate of Secondary Education (CSE), which provides for boys and girls of average ability. Meanwhile, the General Certificate of Education (GCE), which provides the route to university, keeps teachers and taught on a tight rein. Those following CSE courses frequently find themselves more encouraged than their GCE peers to express their own ideas and conceptions, especially in written projects which are evaluated as part of the examining process. The development of mode three examinations has been an especially innovative area of CSE activity, with the teachers in schools devising their own syllabuses and setting and marking the examinations associated with them, the examination boards acting merely as moderators and accreditors.

The opportunity the mode three gives of bringing the ideas and experiences of boys and girls into the examination process was brought home to me during my time as a teacher of economics in a Liverpool comprehensive. Many of those I taught had a closer acquaintance with the nature and priorities of a community whose lifeblood was international trade than would ever fall to me. The economic impact of a dock strike on family life did not have to be explained to them. In producing a CSE mode three syllabus in economics, it was possible to take special account of this. Some of the projects which my pupils presented were a revelation and taught me a thing or two about the ability of young people to think out for themselves the answers to problems which are close to their own experience. And their classroom offerings were an endless source of laughter mingled with pathos. 'Seer', said a fourteen-year-old scouse with a very particular view of the effect of population growth on resources, 'when me mam's in the ozzie having babies, we don't eat – me dad says drinking's more important.'

While the GCE boards insist that many of the modes now available in CSE examinations are the greatest clothes steal since Disraeli dished the Whigs, the CSE has made practices widespread that would otherwise have remained exceptional. For example, the mode two approach, whereby several schools together devise and teach a common syllabus, has existed in GCE circles for a long time, but the advent of the CSE has dramatically increased its use. The reason for this is not hard to see. The CSE has been constructed by teachers. Its subject committees are made up of teachers. Its moderators and examiners are teachers. The CSE puts the examining of schoolchildren where it belongs: in the hands of the teaching profession. Its members decide what is to be taught to children and what form examining and marking will take. By contrast, the GCE is a university construction. Its origins lie in the need to provide a route to a university education. True, it is no longer used exclusively for that purpose, but university requirements still have a good deal to do with the style and content of syllabuses and with methods of examining. The involvement of teachers is of a high order, but the university influence remains immense. It is therefore in no way surprising that there have been few flights by GCE boards into the riskier areas of modern examinationology. For example, it has been left to the CSE boards to experiment with the feasibility of measuring an examinee's performance in a community service activity.

The Metropolitan Regional Examination Board (MREB), which serves the London area, took its courage in both hands in the seventies in accepting a mode three submission from the social education department of my school that was based on the work of the Farmington Trust. The pupils taking the examination concerned spent part of their course helping at local primary schools, old people's homes and day centres for the handicapped. To say the experience they gained of adult roles was a valuable part of their learning experience would be a significant understatement, especially as the young people involved fell into the special category of God's creation that leads some teachers to suppose He did not have them in mind when, as the last verse of the first chapter of Genesis tells us, He looked on everything that He had made, and behold, it was very good. Many of them had achieved very little in their lives, except notoriety for being almost ineducable. But, once placed in situations where they were treated as adults, some – although by no means all – underwent a transformation. Maturity replaced childishness; responsible behaviour replaced irresponsibility; compassion replaced abrasiveness; vision replaced blindness.

Tough little Kay Jones was a changed woman from the day the class she had been working with at the local primary school gave her a book of drawings they had made for her: 'Look, it says *Miss* Jones.' Even more significantly, the headmistress rang up to say what a mature and lively personality she had presented. The dull and childish teenager we knew had undergone a metamorphosis.

Could the examination system do justice to such youngsters without taking into account their attitudes and enactments in curriculum-related community activities? The social educators mounting the programme proposed that 15 percent of the marks for the CSE mode three should be awarded on the basis of an evaluation by supervising staff of pupils' performance in their community service placements. After prolonged negotiations with the MREB, there was a settlement at 10 percent.

The principle thereby established was an important one for the future of the examination system. It would almost certainly have proved impossible to pursue it through any of the GCE boards. Why? Because they specialise in providing for the highly educable, whose best interests are thought to be served by concentration on the academic study of set texts and given propositions rather than experiential learning. Is it not so? 'Why can't we do interesting things like that?' asked one highly academic pupil who had noticed what the social education department was up to. 'Because', came the reply, 'you have got to pass your O levels, so there isn't time.'

The advances achieved by the CSE, if so they be, are likely to be carried into the upper reaches of the ability range if and when the long awaited merger with the GCE O level examination takes place. Meanwhile, it is perhaps not without significance that there will shortly be launched a GCE A level examination in English language. The chairman of the working party responsible for this venture states that it will meet a demand for a syllabus 'that teaches about the significance of language in human thought'. That would seem to have a direct relevance to the business of equipping young people to think for themselves about the information offered to them and about their own experiences.

Outside the confines of examination curricula, young people flex their critical muscles and bring reason to bear on what they often see as the unreasonableness of the structures in which they find themselves. Schools are full of contradictions and one is clearly to be seen in the contrast between the way secondary examinees so frequently accept without question what their teachers offer under the heading of physics or geography or English language, but reject what is dished up in the name of preserving the good reputation of the school.

Soon after the broadcasting of parliamentary proceedings began, Sir Reginald Savoury observed that the interests of the nation would be best served by retaining the House of Lords and abolishing the House of Commons. Quite often, things seem to be happening the wrong way round. Many would welcome the emergence in their examination candidates of a higher critical faculty in the classroom and a lower one outside it.

But despite what has been said so far, the principal cause of the problem identified at the opening of this chapter is neither the difficulty of deciding when children should be encouraged to make their own judgements nor the restrictions placed by the examination system on original thought. The most important factor consists in the different expectations society has of the education system.

There is a significant element in the population firmly of the view that it is the job of schools to repress children's unhealthy disposition to go their own way and decide for themselves what sort of world they want. 'Your job', said Mr Humphries, a parent whose fistic capabilities outreached his mental capacity by about the distance from Manchester to Moscow, 'is to keep the little bleeders down.' While others might not express themselves in quite those terms, many parents look to schools to fit young people to take their place within the existing order of things.

On the other hand, there are those who belong to the Education Liberation Army. While wisely unwilling to meet Mr Humphries in a dark alley at night, they would knock his ideas on the head and probably him as well, given circumstances that offered them a first strike capability. Members of the ELA see education as having to do with the rejection of the outdated *mores* of decaying capitalist society, with its hierarchical structures and puritan work ethic, and the building of a brave new world of egalitarian personhood.

Can an education system cater for both schools of thought? With the polarisation of attitudes that applies in contemporary British society, how is the teaching profession to resolve the dilemma of being faced with contradictory demands? The obvious solution is, of course, to make a simple choice between the two alternatives. There is never any shortage of people in schools prepared to adopt the simplistic approach. One such was the school caretaker in Peter Terson's play about football hooliganism: 'It's the free milk. I wouldn't give them the free milk. It's only the likes of me knows what they do with the dirty straws.' Despite the fact that free milk has disappeared from schools since the National Youth Theatre first stunned audiences with *Zigger Zagger* in 1968, football hooliganism has increased, thereby delivering the death blow to one more uncomplicated and trouble-free solution to human problems.

There is no trouble-free answer to the dilemma facing the teaching profession. The vast middle ground of opinion in society insists on having things both ways. Young people must be made to conform but at the same time encouraged to question. It cannot be otherwise, because our constantly evolving society, of which schools are a microcosm, works upon the same principle.

'To be wise', says Teiresias in *King Oedipus,* 'is to suffer.' When a teacher realises the truth regarding what society expects of schools, immediate and swift escape from the profession might seem the safest course. To repeat what was said in the opening passages of this book: the dichotomy which lies at the heart of a teacher's role makes it inevitable that, whatever approach he takes to a given situation, there will be those ready to applaud and others to attack what he does.

How does all this bear upon the issue of developing in children the power to reason; encouraging them to be critical; equipping them to make their own judgements? The dilemma on whose horns the teacher is painfully perched is made clear by the appeals made to him in this matter. Along with what might be called the Jennings complaint that children are not taught in school to think for themselves, there comes a counterbalancing cry that they are taught to think too much.

It was in the sixties that fear first emerged of young people too much disposed to hold their own views and, most frightening of all, to act upon them. Nothing like it had occurred since Oliver Twist challenged the distribution of resources at the workhouse, for which act of daring, it will be remembered, the member of the governing board in the white waistcoat confidently asserted: 'That boy will be hung. I know that boy will be hung.'

It is not at all unlikely that thoughts of hanging as a suitable disciplinary measure passed through the minds of some of those who suffered the main onslaught of student demonstrations in Europe and America in the sixties. Many occupants of greystone spires – and not a few in redbrick communities and plateglass palaces – believed the end of the world of education as they had always known and loved it was nigh. A decade later, the fear remained. During a sabbatical term at a Cambridge college at the end of the seventies, I was told: 'We were terrified. We could not see where it would end.' Then a question pregnant with anxiety: 'Do you think it could ever happen again?' Something was lost forever in the sixties; or maybe gained, depending how one looks at it. The forces that were released are still at work. The days of the acquiescent undergraduate and the submissive student are probably gone forever. More important for school teachers, the days of the passive pupil are also numbered.

The penultimate Thursday of November in the year 1979 was a sort of landmark in the taking of schoolchildren to the streets. On that day, there was an historic demonstration outside the Department of Education and Science in London, where Under Secretary of State Rhodes Boyson was to be found on the twelfth floor. Children marched in the street below, chanting: 'Two, four, six, eight. We will not amalgamate!' From whence did these young activists come, and by what genus of teacher and parent were they led? What kind of permissiveness had brought them to this place, to be prancing with banners when they might more profitably have been at their books? They were in fact from Highbury Grove School, bastion of Black Paper values, whose corridors had echoed to the feet of Rhodes Boyson as headmaster.

What this illustrates is that progressives and traditionalists alike now accept pupil involvement in policy making as quite proper and acceptable, even to the point of their being party to demonstrations and protests. Within the maintained system, there are few conservatives left in positions of influence. But it would be idle to pretend that the whole of the teaching profession readily accepts the new situation. The very notion of what has from time to time been rather extravagantly referred to as pupil power is an anathema to some, and they will never be reconciled to it. Robert Frost has some relevant lines in his poem *Reluctance*:

> Ah, when to the heart of man
> Was it ever less than treason
> To go with the drift of things,
> To yield with a grace to reason,
> And bow and accept the end
> Of a love or a season?

Massive contradictions emerge as schools explore the new territory in which they find themselves. For example, one suspects that teachers and parents who encourage children to march against local authority decisions on school closures might take quite a different view of boys and girls demonstrating on their own initiative against decisions by their elders in school or at home.

There was an amusing illustration of the inconsistent attitude of adults during a period of industrial action by teachers in the spring of 1982. Children locked out of one school during the lunch hour as a result of staff withdrawn from duties managed to get back in while the premises were empty. When the teachers returned for the afternoon session they found themselves excluded by their pupils. They were, of course, horrified. It was one thing for professionals deliberately to cause distress and inconvenience to those they were commissioned to teach, but quite another if boys and girls responded in like manner. In the young, such practices were indefensible.

Despite the contradictions that are perhaps an inevitable feature of human attitudes and seem to abound among teachers, the eighties witness a fairly wide acceptance of the right of pupils to have a say in school affairs and a part in decision-making. In some local education authorities that even extends to pupil involvement in school government.

Those who maintain their reservations about openness to pupil opinion argue that it leads to indiscipline. There is some justification for that charge. It is not easy for teenagers to accept that participation does not necessarily mean they will have their way. On becoming a headmaster, I asked the sixth form what changes they would like to see for themselves. They immediately came up with two proposals: abolition of prefects and school uniform. I granted both requests, but stipulated that abandonment of uniform would not mean the sixth form being allowed to come to school dressed for a pop festival. Both sexes were forbidden to wear jeans and the young gentlemen were required to wear jackets. There was an immediate protest that without *complete* freedom of dress, the whole exercise was a farce. There was an even more interesting follow-up to my decision that members of the sixth need only attend school when they had lesson commitments on the timetable. Not without difficulty had I persuaded heads of departments this would be a useful preparation for college or university, requiring those concerned to make their own judgements as to the use of time outside lessons. But an ex-pupil who dropped in to discuss the state of the world with his old friends in the sixth later wrote attacking my regime because he found that people were 'unsettled by the freedom'.

Young people are not the only ones who, on being consulted on an issue, assume the final decision will be an unadulterated version of their demands. School staffrooms are full of those who think that being asked what they think means they will get what they want. The same assumption is made in places where industrial democracy is being pioneered. The complaint that there has not been enough consultation has become the standard response to anything short of total victory for the workforce in some sectors. It usually means there has been endless consultation, but that the talking has had to stop and a decision taken.

The most contentious aspect of pupil participation in decision-making is its purpose: one needs to bear in mind T. S. Eliot's warning in *Murder in the Cathedral* against doing the right deed for the wrong reason. In 1972, there was published a book that mightily advanced the case for pupil involvement: *Children's Rights.* Edward Short, who had not long before been Secretary of State for Education, observed that it was 'an impressive onslaught on the savage idiocies with which we as parents and teachers, indeed as a society, hammer our children into our own image'. The contributors to *Children's Rights* included three of the best known advocates of pupil power: Leila Berg, Michael Duane and A. S. Neill. Duane's essay, entitled *Freedom and the State Education System,* argued that schools existed neither to indoctrinate children on the one hand nor simply to teach them to think for themselves on the other. Education existed 'as the means of creating democrats of the future'. Six requirements were laid down as being necessary to the achievement of this purpose:

1   That the society in which and for which the schools exist must itself be democratic, i.e. not divided into separate groups or classes with a relationship of exploitation.
2   That the schools shall be small enough to enable the whole school – staff, parents and pupils – to meet face to face.

3   That schools shall be governed by a joint council of staff, parents and pupils.
4   That the Principal of each school shall be elected for a stated period by the joint council.
5   That there shall be no competitive examinations.
6   That there shall be no system of rewards or punishments.

These requirements call for changes in the structure of society and the organisation of schools that will not come about this side of the final conflict of Armageddon. And, many will say, a good thing too. In order to go all the way with such proposals as these, one must accept the fundamental assumption on which they are based: 'To be democratic is to adopt a way of life so utterly different from what we know in this country that most people are simply unable to envisage not only the forms of work, leisure and sex relationships that would arise, but the valuations, the attitudes and the social relations that would follow.' Not a great many people, and very few teachers, would go all the way with that summary of the Duane doctrine.

Delivering the annual Dimbleby Lecture in the year *Children's Rights* appeared, Lord Annan observed that the most important right of a student was to be well taught. The observation was generally welcomed by teachers, who did not wish to be held responsible for the democratisation of society and who had the gravest doubts about the ways in which it was being suggested that should be brought about. Many held the view that democracy had no more to do with the teaching function of a school than with the navigation of a ship at sea or an aircraft in flight. If a revolution was necessary, which some doubted, schools were not the places from which to launch it.

But that is not to say the majority could not see some less grandiose but better reason to bring young people into the decision-making process in schools. There was in fact a considerable extension during the seventies of elected school councils. The phenomenon was not widespread in primary schools, or such selective schools as survived at secondary level, but was fairly common in comprehensives. Since they were supposed to be in the educational vanguard, it was not altogether surprising that the formalisation of pupil participation advanced most swiftly there.

There is today a wide variety of school councils and similar consultative structures within schools.

What *educational* purpose lies behind the establishment of school councils? They are aimed at helping children to understand the complexities of decision-making and the responsibilities that go along with involvement. They incidentally provide a means whereby pupil opinion may be readily sounded on particular issues, but that is not their principal function and those who say otherwise are misled. Good teachers have never found it difficult to find out what their pupils are thinking. It happens all the time during form time, lessons and out of school activities. If a school needs an elected council to discover what its pupils think about (say) homework arrangements, it has a serious problem in the area of pupil–teacher relationships. Consultative structures that are brought into being to defuse discontent arising from poor communication are educationally indefensible. They may provide a safety valve for unrest, but they obscure a problem that needs to be faced. This was brought home to me by a conversation I had with a comprehensive school headmistress who was having all kinds of pupil unrest following a whole series of staff changes that had brought in its train a major reorganisation of the timetable for the fourth year. 'I have a good mind', she said, 'to set up some kind of council so they have somewhere to moan officially. That might get it out of their systems.' I suggested she might alternatively try explaining the changes to the pupils affected and their parents at an evening meeting. Her response made further advice otiose: 'If we go to those lengths, it will make it look as if something is wrong.'

The creation of a school council should not be seen as a way of avoiding problems. Nor should it be used to give the appearance of participation where none is intended. While it is essential for young people to learn that involvement does not mean they will always get everything they might hope for, it is equally important they do not get the impression of being involved in a charade.

The commonest complaint from those in schools where participation is practised is that the head teacher or some other senior member of staff has the power of veto over whatever the school council decides. That grievance is aired not only by pupils, but also by members of staff. Teachers and taught quickly lose interest in such an arrangement and it is not surprising that some school councils generate about as much enthusiasm as school assembly at nine o'clock on a wet Monday morning or whatever one tries to teach last lesson on a Friday. For a school council to be successful, it must be given some real share in the exercise of power. That being so, it is a matter of critical importance to decide correctly at the outset those matters with which it may properly concern itself. That way, participation may be encouraged without damage to the school as a whole. André Gide has a sentence in *The God That Failed* that seems to me to encapsulate the point: 'Real wisdom consists in listening to opposition views – in fostering them even while preventing them from harming the common weal.'

The genuine educational purpose of a school council is served as much by the continued exclusion of children from some areas of decision-making as their admission to others. It is a poor sort of education that suggests to children that their ideas and opinions are in all things as valuable as those of adults, because it does not equip them with the truth about themselves or the world in which they live. Equally, it is a denial of education to imply that children have nothing of value to offer and that the old edict should still apply about their being seen and not heard. Once again, the extremes are clear and the problem lies in settling the point in between where access should be given to decision-making.

What should be the criteria for admission? Firstly, that the issue at stake is one where children have sufficient knowledge and experience to make a judgement. Secondly, that they are able to accept responsibility for the consequences of whatever decision is made.

The involvement of pupils in deciding school uniform meets both criteria. They know all about the subject; they are perfectly able to take responsibility for a bad decision and live with it for as long as it takes to get it changed. The involvement of pupils in school budgetary policy fails to meet the criteria. The complex factors involved cannot be properly understood by children. More important, it would be impossible for them to accept responsibility for the results of poor distribution of resources: it is something that must remain with professionals.

Since different schools have different styles and priorities, it is altogether logical that they come to different conclusions about what shall and shall not be the territory given over to pupil participation. But some such principles as those mentioned make it possible for a school to have pupil participation that is educationally safe and sound. There are great dangers in departing from them. The involvement of young people in staffing appointments and disciplinary decisions does not advance their education because it gives power without responsibility. The placement of pupils on governing bodies that have power to appoint staff and suspend children is an unsound and alarming development.

It is no service to young people or their better education to pretend they are adults. 'Telling lies to the young is wrong,' writes Yevteshenko. The most important of a child's rights is the right to be a child, free of the responsibilities that come with adulthood. In our concern that young people learn to think for themselves, let us not advance too swiftly the time when the shades of the prison house close upon them.

Five

The Government of Schools

'England', wrote Montesquieu, 'is the freest country in the world.' He spelled out what he believed to be the secret of English liberty in his great work *De l'Esprit de Lois,* published in 1784. The freedom of the Englishman, he observed, derived from the separation of powers between the legislature, executive and judiciary in the government of the nation.

In the two hundred years that have elapsed since Montesquieu made his analysis, political philosophers have frequently declared that the great French jurist was in error. The separation between legislature and executive which he thought he saw did not in reality apply, nor does it today. The effectiveness of the English system of making laws and carrying them out is attributable to the fact that the executive depends upon its majority in the legislature to remain in power.

All of this has a certain relevance to the government of schools, in which there is similarly a separation of powers that is more apparent than real. In the course of an analysis of a teacher's duties in an earlier chapter, reference was made to a requirement laid down in the 1944 Education Act regarding a school's articles of government. These must stipulate the different functions to be performed by the local education authority in whose area the school stands, the governors of the school and the head teacher. Model articles issued by the Ministry of Education the year after the passing of the Act provide the basis for what applies throughout the maintained education system today. A typical division of functions in the running of a school leaves the cake sliced in the following way.

Local Education Authority

The local education authority is responsible for making financial provision for a school and for determining its general educational character within the overall system available in an area.

Governors

The governors are responsible for exercising oversight of the way in which the school is conducted.

Head teacher

The head teacher has control of the internal organisation, management and discipline of the school.

Clearly, this division of functions implies a corresponding separation of powers, making it possible for each element in the triumvirate to proceed without trespassing upon the territory of the other two.

Lying behind this scheme of things are assumptions which, while perfectly valid in the forties, find themselves in an alien world in the eighties. At the time of the 1944 Education Act, the teaching profession was held in much higher regard than today. In particular, the judgement of head teachers in all matters relating to the running of their schools was widely accepted. Decisions about what children should be required to wear, what curriculum they should follow, what examinations they should take, what rewards and punishments should be used to encourage good behaviour and discourage bad, plus a whole host of other decisions associated with these and other aspects of a school's life, were without argument left to the head teacher and his professional colleagues. The governors of a school almost invariably saw their role as a supportive one. By ingenuous expressions of interest in what was going on, they motivated staff and pupils alike, remaining deferential towards the former. The local education authority's responsibility for the general educational character of a school was not seen as going much beyond deciding whether it should be a primary or a secondary school and, if the latter, what place it should occupy within the tripartite system. Given the relationship of trust that existed between the three arms of school government as this country celebrated victory over the Third Reich, the division of functions that applied was perfectly workable. But the alliance has proved as fragile as that which brought victory in war.

It would be difficult to contrive a separation of powers and responsibilities more likely to cause problems in the running of a school today than the inherited arrangements. With the hardening of political stances in educational matters that has taken place in recent years, neither governors nor local education authorities are prepared to maintain a position of non-interference in the details of school organisation, management and discipline. Even more important, the central government is less and less inclined to stand aside from events.

Various influences have brought about the new situation that now obtains. Each goes some way towards explaining why the belief that running schools should be left to professional educators has died the death. *Rigor mortis* having already set in, it would seem worthwhile examining the corpse in order to discern the causes of this fatality.

Firstly, the citizen of the eighties has been encouraged to evaluate and question what is offered to him by way of an education service for his children, a police service for his safety, a medical service when he is sick and a social service when he cannot handle life's problems. No longer does authority of any kind go unquestioned. There now remain few professional groups with the ability to stand aloof from the challenges of the client-consumer. Within the field of education, the new era of accountability has brought the life of a school under keener scrutiny than ever before. On becoming acquainted with curricular policies and classroom practices, people have discovered a good deal to be concerned about. That is not at all surprising, since taking a closer look at almost any part of the social structure inevitably dispels any notions one might have that all is as well as it might be. The stone having been lifted on the education service, all kinds of strange things have crawled out into the light. For example, parents are becoming aware for the first time of the vast discrepancy between the reputation of this or that school and the reality of what happens within it. The resistance to openness presented by some institutions is eloquent. But there can be no turning back to the old way of doing things. Powerful elements within the teaching profession itself have encouraged young people to question authority in all its guises and now that those young people have achieved parenthood, teachers must live with the new situation they themselves have created.

The second influence at work is inseparable from the first, having to do with changed attitudes in the teaching profession. The young teacher of the eighties is a very different creature from someone who entered the profession a sufficient number of years ago to be contemplating surrender to oblivion, sans everything. Consider a man who takes early retirement in 1985 at the age of 57, having entered the profession in 1950 and completed thirty-five years' service. At the time he began to teach, the Prime Minister was Clement Attlee, a man born when Victoria ruled and Gladstone and Disraeli dominated the House of Commons; Winston Churchill had not yet formed his last administration; the President of the United States was Harry S. Truman, who five years earlier ordered the dropping of atomic bombs on Hiroshima and Nagasaki; the leader of the Soviet Union was Joseph Stalin, who knew both Lenin and Trotsky. The Suez Crisis that destroyed Anthony Eden and heralded the Harold Macmillan era had not yet occurred; the election and subsequent assassination of John F. Kennedy were a decade away; a promising young politician named Harold Wilson, recently elected to the House of Commons for the first time, had fourteen years to wait before becoming Prime Minister. A daily newspaper was a copper or two of the old coinage; television was a gadget owned by few; there were no parking problems. Clever children went to grammar schools; handy ones went to technical schools; those neither clever nor handy were dispatched to secondary moderns.

Compare this with the background of a young man about to enter the profession in the mid eighties. As a teenager, he will have seen the end of the Heath and Wilson years and the rise of Thatcherism. He will have entered college as Yuri Andropov came to power in the Soviet Union and Ronald Reagan threatened the deployment of new nuclear weapons in Europe to counterbalance the Russian SS-20 build-up. As a student, his standard of living is far above that his senior colleagues knew after a decade in the profession. If he does not own his own transport already, he very soon will once he begins teaching, thereby adding to the greatest problem facing schools today, which is not how to teach children but where to park all the staff cars. Television keeps him acquainted with the most intimate details of the world's horrors and occasionally a few of its delights. His own education was almost certainly undergone in a comprehensive school. As a result, he is suspicious of anything that smacks of elitism; he abhors hierarchies; he questions what he sees as the despotic power of the head teacher.

In the autumn of 1982, BBC television broadcast a series of programmes depicting life at Kingswood Comprehensive School in Corby. At one point, the headmaster was seen explaining to the English staff why a scale point had been taken away from their department. A young man who appeared to be in but his second year of service to the profession did not mince words in responding: 'You decided this with your cronies.' His view of the upper hierarchy was typical of that held by young teachers today. It is, of course, exacerbated by lack of promotion prospects as the education system contracts. When one can see no way up the mountain, it is all too easy to suspect that those who make it to the higher levels have been shown a secret route or thrown a rope from the top.

The new attitudes that prevail within the lower and middle reaches of the teaching profession towards the power and influence of those above them has played an important part in disturbing the balance of power in school government described earlier. The drive for staff participation in decision-making has added weight to the argument that all kinds of people who were once told to keep their interfering fingers out of the school pudding have a right to help choose the ingredients. Some of those consequently brought into the kitchen have shown a particular enthusiasm for the stirring process.

The third influence at work to bring about change has been the polarisation of views as to what should and what should not be the principal elements in a child's education. It is a question raised more than once already in this book. Does a school exist to pass on certain traditional skills and values or should it encourage children to redesign the world? The answer that it must contrive to do both gives rise to two further issues, both of which caused such public concern in the seventies that there erupted what came to be known as the Great Debate.

The first of the issues had to do with the implications of encouraging children to challenge the existing order of things. Did that not mean organising the teaching process itself with a view to remaking society? Indeed it did, according to those at the forefront of the movement to comprehensivise the education system. In 1970, Caroline Benn and Brian Simon offered the British people a book which listed thirty-one reforms necessary for the reordering of the secondary education system and, in the long-run, society itself. A few examples serve to illustrate the general thrust of the proposals. The allocation of pupils to schools should be handed over to the community; all forms of streaming should be abolished; the GCE O level examination should be put to death, together with Latin as a university entrance requirement; a place in the sixth form should be every pupil's automatic right regardless of his or her previous academic record or intended course of study; a complete reconstruction of the content and method of teacher education should take place to equip the profession for its new role in bringing equality of opportunity to all children and helping to build an egalitarian Jerusalem in this green and pleasant land.

My conviction that the Almighty has a sense of humour was justified by the arrival of Margaret Thatcher as Secretary of State for Education and Science in the year Caroline Benn first made these and similar pronouncements in *Half Way There*. After three years in office, the Minister had this to say to Ronald Butt about what she scathingly referred to as the social democratic view of the educational process:

> It means that, where nature has created great and fundamental differences in abilities, these must not be allowed to determine the individual's chances in life, but rather that society must intervene to restore the balance. It is absolutely appalling. It is so totally opposite to what oneself believes is the job of the

education system, which is to draw out the talents in a child to equip him for life in society. Then it's over to the child to exercise his talent to the benefit of himself, society and his own family.

(The Sunday Times, 8 April 1973)

At its deepest level, the Great Debate was about the issue whose main lines were drawn by the two extremes of opinion just outlined. Was the teaching process an interventionist activity, seeking through its methodologies to change the balance of society, or was its proper concern the development of a child's potential? It is important to observe that the latter interpretation does not preclude the view that schools should encourage young people to think for themselves and perhaps challenge the old social order. However, within that interpretation, self-determination is just one of several talents to be developed: it is not the *raison d'être* of education.

This critical difference of emphasis points to the second issue taken up in the Great Debate of the seventies. If the school's task is both to pass on values and to encourage young people to question them, what should be the balance between the two in the existing condition of society? In a nutshell, *upon what should schools be concentrating their energies here and now?* At that relatively simple level, everyone felt able to join in the discussion.

The debate was fuelled by statements and events that reached downward into the primary schools and upward into the rarified atmosphere of sixth forms. The key word, used in staffrooms and the media to turn the engine of disputation and start things a-roaring, might have been designed for the specific purpose of putting contention on the road. According to one's point of view, *standards* become the boo-word or the hooray-word of the seventies. Its credentials for that dual role were perfect. It had obvious militaristic connotations, raising in the minds of the academic faithful images of flags borne aloft in battle. But for others, its sinister sibilance evoked shadowy powers to be challenged and overthrown.

By the second half of the seventies, the Black Paper had become the bible of those who saw themselves as the watchdogs of traditional academic standards. This brigade of educational guards was led by Professor Brian Cox and Dr Rhodes Boyson, whose *Black Paper 1977* asserted that evidence of declining standards had become overwhelming. Events like the William Tyndale affair seemed to provide evidence that primary education was a disaster area in which progressive methods had denied children the normal reading and writing skills. A Labour Prime Minister, in the person of James Callaghan, raised his voice in support of the view that the education system should put its house in order. On the other side of the argument, freedom fighters Henry Pluckrose and Peter Wilby edited *The Condition of English Schooling,* in which it was claimed that 'not one piece of evidence has been produced to show that standards are declining'.

Whatever the Great Debate failed to do, it established one important fact: education was a legitimate area of interest for any who cared to ask about it or advance an opinion. Like his bank and his doctor's surgery, the school to which a citizen sends his children is no longer the fearful place it once was, where hushed tones and respectful bearing showed a proper gratitude for the granting of an audience. The school curriculum is no more the mystery that once it was. Parents know the difference between streaming and mixed ability, having very likely experienced both. Everyman is an educator.

What remains to be established is the answer to the question to which the public debate on education has been addressing itself – to what end should the main thrust of a school's energies be directed? Put at its simplest level, the divide falls between those who believe a successful school is one that fosters such skills as literacy and numeracy and those who believe academic accomplishments to be far less important than the development of certain attitudes. Of course, every school strives for both, but there is quite often a greater emphasis on one than the other. It is usually revealed not so much by what is said as by the allocation of time and resources. Which side of the divide a school falls will frequently (but not invariably) be determined by the nature of the children it admits. Thus, schools with children of high academic ability have been known to make much of their pupils' academic accomplishments, while those occupied by youngsters with learning problems sometimes under-

line the importance of fostering personal qualities. Said a comprehensive headmaster of my acquaintance whose intake was concentrated almost entirely at the bottom end of the ability range: 'We
don't worry much about academic results here.' In the immortal
words of Mandy Rice-Davies: 'He would, wouldn't he?'

There is at least a case to be made for placing the emphasis the
other way about. Schools with pupils who find learning a straightforward business might reasonably be expected to invest considerable time and effort in fostering personal qualities. Conversely,
those where boys and girls find learning difficult ought, some would
say, to pour all their energies into getting them up to a reasonable
academic standard.

It is perhaps not without significance that, since the education
debate got under way in the seventies, schools in the independent
sector with fine academic reputations have been at some pains to
make known their commitment to fostering activities which
generate a sense of community responsibility. On the other hand,
some of those in the maintained sector renowned for all kinds of
community activities have made great efforts to inform the world of
their belief in the importance of examination results. Few schools
wish to be seen as standing too far from the middle ground between
one kind of emphasis and the other.

Of course, schools have not been the only educational institutions
in which this question of emphasis has been under discussion. I
came across an interesting manifestation of it at University College
London in 1974 at a conference on admissions. The assembled
company of head teachers and sixth-form tutors was assured by a
spokesman for the Faculty of Environmental Studies that its courses
were not too rigorous academically. 'The hard-edged subjects are no
longer compulsory in course options', said Professor D. A. Rurin,
'and this has worked well in terms of staff/student relations.' Then,
almost as an afterthought: 'We have yet to see its effects in terms of
achievement.' I wrote those words down at the time because they so
splendidly represented the spirit abroad in many universities at that
time, where academic standards were lowered in the pursuit of
happy relationships between teachers and taught.

Of the three factors that have delivered the *coup de grâce* to the old division of responsibilities in the running of schools, the last has had the most dramatic effect by encouraging central government involvement in the organisation and management of schools. It is argued that, since the triumvirate of local education authority, governing body and head teacher seems unable in many schools to deliver the educational goods that society requires, the time has come for the Department of Education and Science to take a more active interest in the way they are conducted.

During Question Time in the House of Commons on 16 November 1982, Sir William van Straubenzee asked the Secretary of State for Education and Science whether he would give public access to the contents of reports on schools by Her Majesty's Inspectors and whether he had in mind any proposals for following up such reports. In reply, Sir Keith Joseph said that he had indeed decided to give public access to all reports on formal inspections from 1 January 1983 onwards. He continued as follows:

> We have also decided to introduce more systematic arrangements for ensuring that there is effective follow-up action in relation both to the institutions inspected and, where reports raise matters of wider general application, to other institutions maintained by the local education authority. Action rests in the first instance with the local education authority and governing body of the institutions concerned but we shall be ready to consider what we might appropriately do to assist the local education authority in relation to such action and, in particular cases, to take up Ministerially with the local education authority concerned matters raised by individual reports which are of exceptional concern or importance.

A memorandum was issued by the Department of Education and Science setting out procedural details. The following three provisions were of special interest:

5   A copy of a report issued on a school would in future be sent to the national press and other media, and to the press and media concerned with the area in question.

6   Local education authorities would be expected to meet requests from individuals for copies of a report and to make it available in public places.

8   Her Majesty's Inspectorate would in future publish every six months an appraisal of issues raised in reports 'likely to be of general interest to the education system and its clients.'

A letter to the teachers' associations spelled out what the Secretary of State had in mind with regard to the follow-up to a report. Its implications were disturbing, demolishing the traditional boundaries of central government intervention in the conduct of schools. After the inspection of one of its schools, a local education authority would formally be asked by the Department of Education and Science to consult with the school governors to decide what action to take in view of the findings. Furthermore, local education authorities would be required to report back to the Department within three months as to their intentions. One passage made it clear to those accustomed to reading between the lines that a very high level of intervention would be possible under the new arrangements, notwithstanding the fact that the language of the educational bureaucracy obscured the fact:

It would be for the local education authority to decide what action was appropriate in the light of each report; and how the various aspects of the report's findings should be covered in the reply to the Department. The Secretary of State would wish to know if the local education authority disagreed with the findings so that any such disagreement could be appropriately explored, for example by discussion between HM Inspectorate and the local education authority's professional officers. It would not be appropriate for the Department to seek to monitor in detail the follow-up action undertaken by the local education authority and the institutions it maintains. But the Secretary of State would wish to know, first that, where the local education authority accepted the validity of the report's findings, it was taking appropriate action so that the findings, as far as was practicable, might be applied to improve the quality and effectiveness of education in its area; and, second, what in the opinion of the local education authority the Department might for its part do to assist the local education authority in relation to such action. With these objectives in mind the Secretary of State proposes himself to take up with the local education authority matters arising out of a report which are of exceptional concern or importance.

Most of the public debate about these proposals has been centred upon the question of publishing reports, which is now an accomplished fact, rather than the infinitely more important issue of how they should be followed up. Eric Lord, Chief Inspector at the DES, was given the task of writing to the teachers' unions to assuage their fears about the former. He assured everyone that publication would not change the character of reports. 'We recognise', he wrote conciliatorily, 'that greater public access to reports brings with it the possibility of more people, professional and otherwise, being in a position to debate their findings, and feel sure that from time to time you will wish to take advantage of these opportunities.'

Bernard Levin joined in the debate and gave short shift to those who were, as he put it in *The Times* on 24 November 1982, 'hopping up and down in rage and protest against the suggestion that parents might be told what Inspectors of Schools think of the standards of educational establishments to which they send their children'. His recommended treatment was typically unambiguous: 'The people saying that parents ought not to know what kind of education their children are getting should go and boil their heads.'

To whet the appetite of educational *voyeurs* in preparation for revelations to come, *The Times Educational Supplement* published on the last day of 1982 a report by Her Majesty's Inspectors on a middle school in Hereford and Worcester catering for 180 pupils aged 9 to 12 years. In their concluding remarks, the HMIs were extremely complimentary about the school: the children were well-behaved, lessons carefully prepared and well presented, good standards achieved in English and mathematics and just about everything else except geography and history, where not enough was expected of third formers. There was only one specific proposal made in the report, but it was a highly significant one:

> It is recommended that the school should reconsider the policy of excluding a rather large proportion of pupils from the study of French in the second and third year. Setting by ability, based on progress in learning French in the first year, could enable more pupils to continue this subject throughout their time at the school.

A considerable number of head teachers and modern linguists will have given a wry smile on reading that, as I did. The proposition that setting by ability is the way to give more pupils competence in French constitutes a *volte face* to match Napoleon's retreat from Moscow.

During the seventies, when mixed ability teaching was the fashionable panacea for all educational ills, there was no shortage of support for it among local education authority inspectors. The view of the Inner London modern languages inspectorate was that mixed ability teaching very likely held the key to the wider dissemination of linguistic competence among boys and girls. Indeed, the achievements of the Spanish department in my own school by this method were of such an order that it was used by inspectors as a model for others to emulate. However, less attention was drawn to the German department, where it was a flop. I have found that what matters is not what you do, but the way that you do it. Although no great enthusiast for what goes by the name of educational research, I have read enough of it to know that my opinion in this matter is supported by a good deal of evidence and not least by Neville Bennett's *Teaching Styles and Pupil Progress*. In short, it is not setting or mixed-ability teaching that holds the key to successful teaching, but the individual teacher's belief in the method being used and his or her skill in using it. Like almost everything else I have to say about education, that is a statement of the obvious, and will be recognised as such by members of the profession.

Of course, one need not necessarily suppose that the member of Her Majesty's Inspectorate responsible for the recommendation quoted above held a different view in the seventies, and therein lies a considerable problem. There is frequently no consistency of view between local inspectors and advisers on the one hand and HMIs on the other as to what is and what is not the best way of teaching a subject in a given set of circumstances. That being so, one can see why the Secretary of State's new proposals include a proviso that disagreements between local authority officers and Elizabeth House over the findings of a report shall be 'appropriately explored'. Such explorations are likely to be of great educational value to the different sectors of the inspectorate.

Wider dissemination of the contents of reports on schools and closer central involvement in the follow-up process are the logical outcome of the forces that were at work during the seventies and that continue in the eighties. In view of growing public concern over standards in education, it would have been unthinkable for the Department of Education and Science to have taken no action. Any set of proposals likely to have an effect would be bound to cause apprehension in the teaching profession, since the Great Debate and what has followed from it inevitably reflect upon the competence of those working in the nation's classrooms. But there are dangers ahead and it remains to be seen to what extent DES interference in local education develops in the first half of the eighties. If it does so, the government of schools will head for an even stormier part of the ocean than it presently occupies.

The waves are already high enough to discourage some captains from taking their craft out on fresh voyages. Ask any head teacher who has taken early retirement in the last five years his reason for leaving the profession and the likelihood is he will have something to say about how difficult it has become to do the job in the existing state of school government. Time and again one hears such comments as: 'I can't get out of this soon enough. The job has become impossible.' After making some such observation, a Londoner who was choosing to go in his mid-fifties added a word that will find an echo in many headmasterial hearts: 'Being a headmaster used to be about teaching children. Now it's about politics. Governors' meetings are just open warfare between the factions, with me as everybody's public enemy number one.'

The movement of opinion regarding who should have the major

say in the conduct of a school is well illustrated by the fact that, in his proposals about follow-up action after a report on a school, the Secretary of State made no mention whatsoever of the head teacher. The DES will 'request the local education authority, in consultation with the governors of the inspected institution, to consider, having regard to the statutory responsibilities of each party, what action is required. . . .' The third party in the traditional triumvirate of school government is ignored. Whether the result of an oversight or by deliberate design, the absence of any reference to the involvement of the head teacher in consultations arising from the inspection of his or her school signals a dramatic departure from past practice.

The erosion of the power and influence of the head teacher has been one of the most notable developments of recent years. As education has been placed more and more in the centre of both local and national political debate, old assumptions have been cast aside and new questions asked. In particular, the definition of powers described at the beginning of this chapter has come in for very close scrutiny. As a result, the conflict between the right of a local education authority to determine the general educational character of a school and the head teacher's responsibility for its organisation, management and discipline has been highlighted. Similarly, the nature and extent of the oversight to be exercised by governors has become an issue of major importance.

A schoolboy, on being asked to tell all he knew about Socrates, wrote: 'Socrates was a Greek. He asked questions. They poisoned him.' The asking of questions about school government that no one in the past thought it polite or necessary to raise has poisoned the old relationship between the three parties involved. For example, once school governors began to inquire as to precisely what they were supposed to be overseeing, and by what means, and to what end, many a storm broke. Again, once the elected members of a local education authority began to ask about the precise methods by which head teachers conducted their schools and then to pass resolutions defining how they should or should not do so, the old order of relationships could not survive. The compulsion felt by many local politicians to rule upon the use of corporal punishment in schools illustrates the new forces which have been released in council chambers. Anyone who thinks local councillors are going to be happy to stop at prohibiting one particular sanction is blind to the obvious. If the cane can be abolished at a stroke, so to speak, what further challenges might be mounted against the entrenched reactionary power of the teaching profession?

The Taylor Report, published in the autumn of 1977, pointed the direction which school government has since been taking. Almost half the twenty members of the Taylor Committee were local politicians and education officers, and their findings reflected the county hall view that the power and influence of head teachers should be reduced. Significantly, the committee included only four members of the teaching profession.

There are three key paragraphs in the Taylor Report that make clear the committee's intentions for the future control of schools. Each seeks to transfer power from the head teacher to the governing body. Taken together, these paragraphs provide the basis for an entirely new way of conducting a maintained school from what has generally obtained in the past:

5.29   The nature of the relationship between the school and parents to be set down in a letter sent by the governors to those accepting places for their children.

6.23   Concerning the school curriculum, the governors to be given responsibility by the local education authority 'for setting the aims of the school, for considering the means by which they are pursued, for keeping under review the school's progress towards them and for deciding on action to facilitate progress'.

6.33   Concerning behaviour and discipline, and within the context of the local education authority's general policy framework, the governors to be given responsibility 'for formulating guidelines which promote high standards of behaviour and for making such minimum rules and sanctions as are necessary to maintain such standards in the school'.

In all three of the areas of responsibility dealt with in these clauses, it has traditionally been the head teacher and his professional colleagues who take the lead and make the decisions. One of the most important functions of a headmaster or headmistress in the past has been communicating to the parents of new pupils the relationship it is hoped to foster with them; curriculum and teaching methods have been the province of the professionals; standards of behaviour and their enforcement have been teachers' territory. In those places where the Taylor proposals are being implemented, governors' oversight of schools has taken on an entirely new dimension and the responsibility of head teachers for the internal organisation, management and discipline of their schools is being effectively removed.

The teaching profession can take little comfort from the fact that the Education Act of 1980 left a good deal of Taylor to gather dust upon the bookshelves at the Department of Education and Science, along with all the other reports that have gone that way this century. There are two reasons why teachers have cause to be concerned about the Taylor proposals.

Firstly, although they may not have done a great deal to change the letter of school articles of government, the proposals have dramatically changed the spirit in which many governors meet. Where the local councillors and their nominees, who dominate many governing bodies, would once have been reluctant to lay down the law about the curriculum and teaching methods, deferring to the head teacher, that is no longer always the case. Even more important, it is becoming quite common to hear stories of staff appointments being made against the wishes of head teachers, sometimes deliberately in order to introduce a challenge to the existing style in which a school is conducted. A head teacher recently approached me for advice about this. He said: 'I have had someone planted on my governors to stir up trouble and give me staff who are hostile. Is that allowed?' Sadly, the answer is that it is not only allowed but encouraged in some local education authorities, including the largest, richest and most powerful, from which the story comes.

Secondly, while the 1980 Education Act fell a long way short of implementing Taylor, it left the way open for local education authorities to do so if they wished. It did so by leaving unaltered the arrangements whereby the functions to be exercised by the three traditional elements in school government – local education authority, governors and head teacher – are determined by articles drawn up by the first named. Any local council that chooses to implement clauses 6.23 and 6.33 of the Taylor Report is free to do so, thereby making it explicit that local politicians instead of professional teachers shall determine the subjects to be taught in its schools, the teaching methods to be adopted, the behavioural attitudes to be fostered and the disciplinary sanctions to be employed. True, it has not happened yet, but few members of the educational *cogniscenti* would say other than that there are local education authorities within which a significant group would like to see it. Is it not so?

It has been argued that giving more power to governing bodies in the way suggested by Taylor would not mean greater political control of schools, because of the accompanying proposals about membership. The appointment of equal numbers of local education authority representatives, school staff, parents and representatives of the local community as governors of a school appears to constitute a safeguard against increased politicisation. But the likelihood is that political people will continue to dominate since Taylor specifically proposes that local councillors shall be eligible in two categories: as local authority nominees and as local community representatives. Furthermore, the responsibility for drawing up a list of people suitable for co-option should, says Taylor, rest with the local education authority. Taylor's intentions are as plain to see as Wackford Squeers' incompetence at spelling.

Despite all that has been said so far, there is one respect in which the voice of the professional teacher is growing in strength in the places where decisions are made about the running of schools. The drive to reduce the authority of head teachers has had great support in the lower echelons of the teaching profession, to considerable effect. The inclusion of staff representatives on governing bodies is probably not the most important consequence of the popularisation of the gospel of participation. Far more significant has been the extent to which head teachers have introduced consultative structures within the organisation of their schools. Thus, while the views of what might be called the top professional in a school's teaching force are not respected as once they were, those of the bottom professionals are ignored at everyone's peril.

I was extremely surprised to be appointed a head teacher in 1970 at the age of 36, but I think I know which of my statements at interview turned the scales in my favour. 'I am', I said, in answer to a question about making decisions, 'a consultation man.' The effect upon the governors, not to mention the inspectors and administrators of the Inner London Education Authority who were present to advise them, was magical. Looking back, I think I missed my opportunity to ask whether a limousine and chauffeur went with the appointment. I am convinced I would have got both.

That was more than a dozen years ago, and the belief that head teachers should and must consult their colleagues before making decisions has taken a firm hold generally and an unbreakable grip in the capital city. William Stubbs, who succeeded Peter Newsam as Education Officer for the Inner London Education Authority (ILEA) in 1982, wasted no time in declaring his commitment to the concept and to that of power sharing by head teachers. Before the year was out, he had told a seminar on headship organised by the Centre for the Study of Comprehensive Schools:

> The trail-blazing head teacher, committed to leading from the front, is not wanted in London schools. It is more and more now a team approach in schools. The idea of there being a team leader who can carry the whole school forward – I'm sorry, I don't see it.

Appropriately enough, *The Times Educational Supplement* of 3 December 1982 reported this statement under the heading: *ILEA Seeks New Breed of Head Teacher*. Charismatic leadership no longer has a place in Inner London schools. Although preposterous, that was to be expected. It is preposterous because leadership from the front is quite obviously necessary in certain school situations and there are many teachers who prefer it to being shoved from the back into the participation pantomime; but it was to be expected because it was foreshadowed as long ago as 1974 when an ILEA working party on school government asserted that leaving head teachers with ultimate responsibility for running schools was not an arrangement to be regarded as immutable. The day might come when school articles of government would 'place the balance of responsibility elsewhere'.

I recollect my first experience of prizegiving at the prestigious London grammar school where my own teaching career began a quarter of a century ago. 'We will now', said the chairman of governors, 'have a vote of thanks proposed by the School Capting.' He pronounced the *g* with careful emphasis. 'After that', he added, continuing to enunciate with care, 'we will have the Vice-Capting.' Despite lacking an absolute command of English, the distinguished alderman in question was a splendid servant of the school, deeply respected by staff and pupils alike and regarded with great affection. He knew his limitations and was happy to leave designing the curriculum and getting the boys to conduct themselves in a civilised manner to those who were qualified to deal with just such things. In the conditions of today, he would have stood no chance of being appointed to be chairman of the governing body of any school in the state sector.

Opinion within the teaching profession as to whether the government of schools is moving in the right direction is not clearly formulated. That is in part because many teachers still have very little knowledge of the powers and responsibilities of governors, and even less of the changes taking place as these words are written. Those with most to lose as the old separation of powers gives way to something new are head teachers, whose ability to shape the schools they are supposed to be running becomes increasingly difficult. But they are also the ones who stand to gain most from the radicalisation of school government, for they cannot forever be held responsible for things over which they have no control.

Montesquieu's complimentary remarks about the government of England followed a visit to these islands in 1729 which gave him such pleasure that he stayed for two years. He at one time observed with great approval in his *Travel Notes* that 'the sovereign, whose person is controlled and limited, is unable to inflict any imaginable harm on anyone'. Whether circumscribing the powers of head teachers to the same degree will in the end prove beneficial to children remains to be seen.

Six

Religion in Schools

Having discussed the government of schools, this is the logical point at which to include a brief chapter on the one subject in the school curriculum which is included by force of statute, *viz* religion. Its unique place in our education system has become increasingly paradoxical in recent years, creating problems which cannot be ignored in any attempt to analyse the condition of teaching.

There is a poignant moment in Tom Kempinski's play *Duet for One* when the leading character, a woman once destined for fame as a concert violinist but confined to a wheelchair by paralysis, cries out in hopelessness: 'There isn't a god, but you can see where they got the idea from.' Religion, some would say, is the ultimate case of necessity mothering invention. It is the only subject in the school curriculum whose basic assumption is of questionable validity.

No one would argue that mathematics is not a proper study for children, asserting that numbers do not exist; no one would suggest that history has no place in school, insisting that the events of the past did not occur; no one would dare to confront the physical education specialists in a school with the proposition that the human physique was a figment of the imagination.

Of course, one may argue about what sort of mathematics to teach children and what methods to adopt. At university level, questions may even be raised as to the invariable application of mathematical laws. An Oxford entrance paper in philosophy once asked whether it was possible to imagine a world in which two plus two did not equal four. But the very asking of such a question at that level in itself demonstrates the fundamental assumption behind the teaching of mathematics in schools, which is that numbers exist and bear relationships to one another that remain constant.

94

In a similar way, one may argue about what history to teach children, even to the extent of challenging the view that something happened the way the text books say, but without throwing aside the fundamental assumption that our forbears actually lived. Whatever Henry Ford may have meant by his remark in 1919 that history is bunk, it cannot have been that the 1914–18 war did not occur. What his words are most frequently taken to mean is that some of the lessons history appears to teach us are misleading.

In the area of historical interpretation, there will always be endless arguments, which become more intense the higher one moves up the academic ladder. In the first half of this century, there was a great deal of debate among our most eminent historians as to the extent to which history was a science. As the century began, York Powell, the Regius Professor at Oxford, made a confident assertion about the nature of his subject: 'It deals with the condition of masses of mankind living in a social state. It seeks to discover the laws that govern these conditions.' In the preface to his great *History of Europe,* published in 1934, H. A. L. Fisher offered an alternative view: 'Men wiser and more learned than I have discerned in history a plot, a rhythm, a predetermined pattern. These harmonies are concealed from me. I can see only one emergency following upon another as wave follows upon wave, only one great fact with respect to which, since it is unique, there can be no generalisations, only one safe rule for the historian: that he should recognise in the development of human destinies the play of the contingent and the unforeseen.' After the war against Hitler, A. L. Rowse offered a middle way. In the introduction to his *Use of History,* he observed that natural science has loosed huge forces upon mankind – an observation that has grown hideously in its significance since it was made in 1946. The ability to control those forces, he insisted, depended to no small degree on developing the social sciences: 'The bed out of which all the social sciences spring is history; there they find, in greater or lesser degree, subject-matter and material, verification or contradiction. There is no end to what we can learn from history, if only we will, for it is conterminous with life. Its special field is the life of man in society and at every point we can learn vicariously from the experience of others before us in history.'

The differences of opinion between historiographers about the nature and purpose of their subject in no way reduce its validity as a proper area of study for school children; they in fact do the opposite. The attempt to make sense of the events of the past and to decide what particular kind of sense one is talking about while making that attempt, merely serves to underline the unarguable fact that the past actually occurred and is a legitimate area of study.

Physical education provides a third example of the principle under discussion. Here again, there may be arguments about how it should be provided and even whether or not young people should be made to do it by their schools when they are beyond the statutory leaving age, but the existence of the human physique is not in question. It is perhaps worth noting in passing that the debate among physical education specialists in recent years has been closely related to comprehensivisation of the education system. Where once secondary schools tended to concentrate on the development of physical skills in those blessed with an abundance of them, there is now much greater emphasis on seeing to it that all children reach their potential, including those for whom any form of physical activity is about as appealing as the offer of a deck-chair to someone stranded in the middle of the Sahara. But the suggestion that participation in physical education lessons should be optional does not derive from doubts about the validity of the subject, but from differences of opinion about its alleged benefits.

Religious education is a different saucepan of herrings from any other subject in the school curriculum, since the vast majority of the population lives in accordance with the assumption that religious belief is unjustified. Most adults have little or no contact with the activities by which it is the normal practice to acknowledge a god, namely prayer and worship. Of course, a good many people would claim to be Christians, asserting by word or lifestyle that it is possible to be nearer to God in a garden – or when cleaning the car or going for a trip to the coast – than anywhere else on earth, but they do not, in fact, use those activities for religious purposes. If it is even half way to being true that by their deeds ye shall know them, it is abundantly clear that most citizens of the United Kingdom today deny the existence of a deity. Paradoxically, the principal exceptions are to be found among those racial groups which have migrated to this country in the last half-century from places we colonised in the heyday of the church. But the most devout of them are not Christians but Hindus and Moslems.

The peculiar position in which religion finds itself in schools is exacerbated by the fact that it is the only subject included in the curriculum by force of law. Nor does the 1944 Education Act stop at the requirement that religion be part of the timetable of lessons; it goes on to insist that the school day should begin with an act of worship, thereby calling upon teachers and pupils alike to perform a rite of belief.

In order to come to terms with the extraordinary contradiction between what most adults actually think of religion and what schools are required by law to teach children, the education system has adopted two strategies. Firstly, the religious education sylla- buses designed by local education authorities have come to place increasing emphasis on the social outworkings of religious belief rather than its substance. Secondly, morning assembly has replaced morning worship.

The movement away from simply teaching children scripture was dramatically accelerated in the mid-sixties by the appearance of a book which challenged the very assumption on which a good deal of religious education was built, namely that Bible stories provided the right foundation for religious understanding. Ronald Goldman's *Readiness for Religion* struck many RE specialists like a thunderbolt. Could it possibly be true, as he asserted, that young children were quite incapable of comprehending what the Bible had to say, and that teachers had been fooling themselves for years? While Gold- man's proposition spread a good deal of alarm and despondency among conservative RE teachers, his message lent support to those in the profession who were becoming increasingly disturbed by the requirements of the 1944 Act. Goldman undoubtedly overstated his case and the swing away from the use of biblical material has since been reversed; but the emphasis in religious education has changed permanently. In short, what boys and girls are taught today has little to do with what to believe about the Bible and everything to do with how to behave towards those around them. Scripture has given way to social studies; the ten commandments have given way to situation ethics.

The beginning of the school day reflects similar trends. No longer will a visitor to a school find himself listening to a scripture reading when the pupils assemble. In most secondary schools the singing of hymns has gone as well. Participatory homiletics rule. They are based upon passages and stories from a vast range of sources, many of them with little or nothing to do with religion. Faced with the choice between a daily act of hypocrisy and a daily act of something other than worship, head teachers have chosen to abandon the former and settle for presenting something they can live with inside themselves. The fact that statutory requirements are thereby not enforced disturbs few consciences, since the religious clauses of the 1944 Education Act are regarded in today's multi-ethnic, pluralist society as a case of the law being a considerable ass. There is a strong feeling in some quarters that the clauses should in fact be repealed. But the arguments against such a step are powerful ones.

Firstly, it is important that children and young people should be educated in the religious area of life. Man is a religious animal. His religious beliefs have frequently dictated the path of history. The institutions he has constructed to organise, control and give expression to religion are some of the most powerful on earth. Professor T. E. Jessop has summarised the position: 'When we look over the past and over the whole earth at present we find that it is religion that is normal and the lack of it that is exceptional. There has never been a whole people without a religion and there is not now. When the non-religious man is seen against the background of the world and of history he appears as an exception.'

The education system would clearly be in default if it omitted to provide children with a knowledge and understanding of religion. But that is not, some would say, an argument for making it compulsory by law. The answer is that to change that situation now would be tantamount to making an official government announcement that the religious era in human history was over and that it was time for mankind to move on from that particular piece of nonsense as surely as he once moved on from the idea that the world was flat. In short, to repeal the religious clauses of the 1944 Education Act would be to make an appallingly misleading statement.

But that is not to say the clauses should be left untouched, nor religious education as it is practised left unchanged. Two developments are desirable.

Firstly, the requirement that each school day should begin with an act of worship should be abolished. It is one thing to teach children the facts of religion; it is quite another to demand that they behave as if they actually possess religious belief. It is a paramount religious truth that one man's faith cannot be instilled in another. The pilgrimage to belief is the most individual of all human activities. I believe only when *I* believe. That being so, it is unthinkable that one human being should require another to believe as he does or act as if it were so.

Secondly, we should sort out what it is we expect teachers of religion to offer children. At the moment, there is a polarisation of opinion which creates immense problems for teachers and taught. In one camp, there are those who yearn for the good old days of straight scripture, taken neat without being diluted by reservations about the existence of a god or the authority of the Bible. In the other, there are those who see religious and social studies as a sort of all-purpose combined camping and first-aid kit for journeys into the unknown. I know a young teacher of the second kind who introduces herself to her thirteen-year-olds with some such statement as: 'I don't myself believe in a god, but you will find what we are going to do helpful in deciding how to treat other people as you make your way in life.'

In the last decade or two, investigations into what should or should not be the content and style of religious education have blossomed like daffodils in spring or spots during a bout of measles, depending on how you regard the results. Perhaps the time has now come for a climactic government inquiry, with proposals for a radical reappraisal of the whole question. Seeing how unusual it is for me to go in for such fashionable phraseology as that, you will appreciate how seriously I regard this issue.

Seven

Classroom Styles

From late July to early September, teachers provide the rest of the population with the excuse it needs for underpaying its educators. The prospect of having to look after the children they brought into the world is grim enough under normal circumstances for many parents; the horrific reality of having them about for six or seven weeks makes solitary confinement in a soundproof cell an attractive proposition. The enthusiasm of the younger generation for pop records, played at a sufficient volume to reach life on other planets, presents a particular problem. 'The hols are alive', wept Jilly Cooper in *The Sunday Times* one August, 'with the sound of music.'

But for teachers, the summer recess is a time when their thoughts and feelings undergo a three-stage process of regeneration. Firstly, they recover from the effects of the academic year just ended. Secondly, they reflect on the possibility of making a living in a manner less likely to bring an early death (teachers have more heart attacks than the members of any other profession). Finally, they turn their minds to a new school year in which, given a reasonable amount of help from Out There, children will be attentive, parents appreciative and salary negotiations completed a week or two before the award is rendered worthless. To understand how teachers annually arrive at stage three every September it is necessary to appreciate that they are the most unshakably optimistic bunch of people in the kingdom. It stands to reason that it must be so, for who but one within whose breast hope eternally springs would contemplate the task a teacher attempts to perform?

For about six hours each day, a primary school teacher attempts to generate interest in a variety of different subjects within the class for which he or she is principally responsible. For the same amount of time, a secondary school teacher strives to arouse the enthusiasm of several different classes in one subject. The two tasks, while not identical, have a common problem: within any one class, there are varieties of ability, disposition and experience. The streaming *versus* unstreaming debate sometimes leads attention away from the fact that every class is a mixed ability class, not to mention a mixed aptitude class and a class in which the quality of life outside school is different for every child. It is a platitude that every young person is a unique individual, but one all too easily buried by institutional necessity. Indeed, it is hardly possible to run a school without subjugating individuality to the common weal. Without some form of categorising children, it would not be possible to organise classes, prepare children for this or that examination, decide who shall study which subjects or settle any of the other multitude of things necessary to establish arrangements that make teaching possible in the form in which it is practised in the maintained system.

The impossibility of the teacher's task becomes clear when one gives proper consideration to these matters. Whether in the primary or secondary sector, a classroom practitioner is called upon to control, stimulate and educate one or more gatherings of thirty children from nine o'clock in the morning to four o'clock in the afternoon, five days a week, taking account of differences within and between groups as to each individual's age, sex, ability, background, lifestyle, attitude, academic record and inclination to get up in the mornings in time to have breakfast. I once knew a mathematics teacher who kept a supply of extremely stale biscuits for those who came to school on empty stomachs. Any unbreakfasted boy or girl who arrived for first lesson feeling queasy and asking to be excused was promptly presented with one of these biscuits. Faced with Mr Taplow's solution to morning hunger, most children rose early on days when he was teaching them.

Seeing what children are like, and bearing in mind what is required of those who embark upon a career devoted to teaching them, it is not surprising the profession is filled with extraordinary characters. Indeed, it is hardly possible for someone to teach effectively unless he or she be somewhat out of the ordinary. The best classroom practitioners are larger than life; their influence is felt even when they are not physically present; their impact remains with those they teach for a lifetime. I recollect a staffroom discussion when we were yarning about those who had taught us in our school days. One colleague told us how her favourite teacher was transformed into a raging monster by the sight of anyone leaning against a wall. 'To this day', she admitted, 'I can't bring myself to lean against anything.'

Teaching is a form of acting. It is you at the front, and thirty of them, and the door shut. Often, the part one plays spills over into private life and it is necessary for one's family or acquaintances from the real world to haul down the curtain with some such remark as: 'You're not in school now, you know.' I remember seeing a film years ago called *A Double Life* about a stage actor who carried whatever role he happened to be playing into his private life. That was all very well when he was cast in a comedy, but it had disastrous results when he took the lead in *Othello*. Assuming the personality of the jealous moor offstage, he committed a murder to match that of Desdemona. Teachers should be the last ones to scoff at such fantasies. Put a bunch of them together for an evening and they play up to one another as if a talent scout from the National Theatre were hiding in the woodwork.

Dame Sybil Thorndike once observed: 'You are never too old to play St Joan. You're only too young.' I once heard a college lecturer insist that young teachers were, of course, much more able to communicate with teenagers than older ones. The reason? Being near to the ages of their pupils, they understood them better. That is the kind of bland assertion that looks alright at a safe distance, which is where the speaker was careful to keep himself in relation to the classroom, but is known to be nonsense by experienced practitioners. True, young teachers of high quality make their own special contribution to the intricate signalling network through which staff and pupils communicate with one another in a school, but in my experience that has little to do with age and a great deal to do with natural talent. What Dame Sybil had to say about acting applies to teaching: experience is the basis of success in the most important roles. It is necessary to make this point because the view is often expressed that one is either a natural teacher or one is not, and no amount of training can make much difference to most individuals. Like the majority of generalisations, that is true only at the extremes.

The person with a mountain of innate ability as a teacher is going to be good at it whatever happens. It is both a delight and a discouragement to the rest of us, as we look back on our own early struggles, to see such precocious skill in action. I recollect watching one winter morning a young woman in her early twenties handling with consummate skill a group of teenagers who would have put fear into the heart of Genghis Khan. It was morning break and they were supposed to go outside but, should they contrive to give young Miss Jenkins the slip, there was every prospect of staying in for a quick puff in the toilets. With a mixture of firmness, wit and manipulative skill, the teacher shepherded the whole group out. 'I wish', said one of my deputies (comprehensives are oversubscribed in that department if no other), 'I could have done that at her age.' Then he added: 'But, of course, some of that lot know her in the classroom.' It was a significant afterthought. A teacher who can perform effectively on the main stage of education rarely has trouble in the wings.

It is equally the case that someone with no natural aptitude for teaching cannot be turned into an effective practitioner, though he be sent on the most carefully constructed training courses in the kingdom, offered more rules of guidance than are found in the pentateuch and permitted to remain in the profession year upon year in the hope that experience will somehow do the trick. Sadly, there are those operating in schools today whose professional history matches that description. Such a man was Mr Edwardson, whose attempts to teach geography to secondary school pupils were, in the words of one of his more outspoken colleagues, 'good material for a horror film'.

In between the Miss Jenkinses of the profession and the Mr Edwardsons come the rest of us. With sound training and a good deal of experience, the majority of those who set foot in the profession are able to make a fair shot at pedagogy, given a little help from their friends, by which I mean not only their colleagues but, more importantly, their pupils. Most teachers discover fairly quickly that children are friendly, supportive creatures, who wish to help. The awful notion that young people are ill-disposed towards adults in general and their teachers in particular, so prevalent in the sinister sixties and encouraged by the media with lip-smacking relish as bigger and better confrontations took place, was a misunderstanding of almost catastrophic dimensions.

The belief that the natural condition of any two adjacent generations of the human race is that of being in conflict with one another in an endless nuclear war seems dangerously close to being taken for granted. 'We don't expect to be able to talk to her,' said two dispirited parents whose daughter was causing problems at home and at school. Pressed by me as to why that was, they looked surprised. 'Well,' said father, 'that's the way it is, isn't it?' But as many parents and teachers are able to testify, that is not the way it is. It is not written in the stars that communication between sixteen-year-olds and forty-year-olds cannot be; it is not against the laws of nature for the generations to enjoy one another's company. The great majority of young people in this country love their parents and like going to school. That is an assertion based not upon sociological research but a quarter of a century's experience of working with boys and girls. Perhaps someone ought to make a television programme about it.

It is the help and support of children that turns most entrants to the profession into effective teachers. Given a certain amount of forbearance on the part of our pupils as we learn to control our classes, organise our teaching material, write on the blackboard, mark a school register, correct exercises, adjust to different ages and abilities in moving from class to class and the multitude of other things that go to make the life of a teacher, we will survive and prosper. Looking back on my own early teaching career, and especially the shattering experience of moving from a boys' grammar school into a mixed comprehensive, it is a wonder to me that my ignorance and incompetence did not bring terrible retribution from those placed in my incapable hands. One of the problems I find today as a BEd teaching-practice examiner is that children make such efforts to help even the most awful students that it is difficult to make an accurate assessment.

Given adequate training, experience and help, what does the average teacher become? In the acting profession, certain histrionic styles are well known. No one could confuse the Olivier manner with the Brando method. It is similarly possible in the teaching profession to identify certain pedagogic styles quite clearly. Most teachers in due course adopt one or other of these to a greater or lesser degree.

The Undertaker

This type of teacher is a dour character, or so appears. The *Daily Express* cartoonist Giles depicts him from time to time, looking like a funeral consultant who has just climbed out of one of his coffins. Monday mornings are for him the best of times and the worst of times. He is in his element in the staffroom, deploring the very fact that Monday has come. If it is not raining already, he knows for sure it will be wet by break time. As the week proceeds, his gloom increases to match his conviction that his pupils become more ignorant with each day that passes. On Thursdays, he can barely bring himself to contemplate what lies ahead for, even should he arouse some spark of interest in his charges, there is yet the profoundly depressing prospect of Friday to be endured. His normal reaction to any suggestion for a change of policy that might improve things is to shake his head and assert: 'It won't work. We tried that before.'

As a young teacher, I worked in a school where there was an undertaker on the staff. His subject was history and, since it was also one of mine, I was permitted to watch him at work in the classroom. The suggestion was not, of course, his. He promised me a gloomy experience. But the head of history, who was intent on making a schoolmaster of me, made a different forecast. He predicted that I would see something of infinite value, and so it turned out. Mr Graves foreseeably carried his sad countenance and poor opinion of his pupils, the education system and the world at large into the classroom. At the outset of the lesson he made an announcement: 'Someone has come along to watch you at work this afternoon. He'll be lucky if he sees anything worthwhile here, won't he?' To a man, his charges gave the required response: 'Yes sir!' They did so with great cheerfulness and it was clear from the start that teacher and taught had a first-class relationship with one another. During the next three-quarters of an hour, I got to the bottom of Mr Graves. He was the classroom equivalent of the comedian whose technique hangs upon the exploitation of his miseries. One such named Les Dawson recently stated that he was not at all put down by the economic recession because, unlike everyone else, he was a failure in the boom years. It was the sort of remark Mr Graves would have made, and I can even hear the tone of voice he would have used.

The Archaeologist

The book of Ecclesiastes has some advice for the archaeologists of the profession: 'Say not thou, "What is the cause that the former days were better than these?" for thou dost not inquire wisely concerning this.' The archaeological approach to education is that which constantly affirms the need to dig up and restore the conditions of the past. As the book of Ecclesiastes also says, there is no new thing under the sun, and the desire to return to the old ways in education did not originate in this century. To take but one example, the demise of corporal punishment was being used to explain hooliganism as long ago as 1899, and its restoration proclaimed as the remedy for truancy. In that year, R. C. Lindsay had this to say on being installed as head teachers' president:

> The appearance of the 'Hooligan' has turned attention to the weakness of our compulsory attendance regulations; and the caprice and carelessness of the Magistracy in dealing with refractory parents. That the blame of all juvenile offences and irregularities should be credited to the school is a public libel against a body of patient, self-sacrificing, and Christian workers. If there be, and I think there is, less respect shown to superiors than formerly, less courtesy and gentleness towards others, less obedience to parents and teachers, the fault lies not at the teachers' door, but springs from the mock sentiment and cant that prevail regarding corporal punishment. The proverb

'Spare the rod and spoil the child' never required to be more loudly proclaimed than today.

(*The Head Teacher,* 14 January 1899)

I quote that passage not to make any point about caning, on which subject teachers' opinions will forever remain divided, but to illustrate the fact that yearning for the past existed within the profession half a century before the 1944 Education Act. It has, of course, massively increased in volume in recent years, not least through the publication of Black Papers that have converted the resurrection of the old into a systematic and recognisable educational philosophy.

There is something of the archaeologist in almost all teachers, many of whom are also parents, which powerfully concentrates their minds on what the profession ought to be up to. It would be my guess that half those working in schools today would like to see more time given to teaching basic skills; more emphasis placed on good conduct; more respect demanded for authority.

The fully committed archaeologist does not beat about the bush whether addressing colleagues or parents. Miss Digwell was such a one, never failing to offer the same observations to all and sundry year after year concerning the eleven-year-olds she received from local primary schools. Their English was poor because they had never been taught to spell or write sentences properly; nor had they been taught their mathematical tables; worst of all, they were like wild animals, discipline having gone the way of the dodo in every corner of the education system except Miss Digwell's own class-room. Her confident annual assertion that her new class was even worse than the one before would have seemed extremely bleak had it not been for her determination to put things right. Archaeologists not only know what is wrong with the education system: they set about remedying things in the part of it where they have control. They roll up their sleeves and get down to basic spadework with a will.

Archaeologists are extremely popular with school caretakers, who are generally of the view that children today are allowed far too much freedom, beginning with their being permitted to exist at all.

One can understand their point of view, since it is obvious schools would be much easier to maintain and keep clean if boys and girls were not constantly tramping about in them. There was an Irish school caretaker in Liverpool who would sometimes come to me towards the end of the morning on a wet and muddy day and ask, 'Sor, could ye not give the kids the afternoon off, and save me a lot of work?'

The Hero

When President John Fitzgerald Kennedy was asked how he came to be a naval war hero, he said: 'It was involuntary – they sank my boat.' There is a heroic style of teaching that is based upon giving children the impression that one has seen the world, done great deeds, known and conquered fear in situations that can only be hinted at and been involved in events of such importance as to make it a privilege for children to be granted the benefit of one's presence in the classroom. At its most sophisticated, this style is presented in the self-denigrating manner of JFK.

I had a colleague who had seen service in a fighter squadron during the war who managed to convey the impression that he had won the Battle of Britain single-handed. Sometimes in the summer he would wear a blazer with his old squadron badge on it. But the hero's guise these days is usually that of sportsman or sportswoman; now and again it is that of pop musician. He who has performed great sporting feats on distant fields; she who has wielded racket or stick on the nation's behalf; they who have plucked guitar strings at gigs listed in *Time Out* – these are today's heroic ones who carry into the classroom vibrations from another world, so that children feel themselves to be having close encounters of the fourth kind.

Most staffrooms have a hero: someone with a claim to local or national fame. A school without should manufacture one, for he or she plays an important part in promoting the image of teachers as people capable of coming to something in the real world. A distinguished headmaster of today who was once my deputy spent a year or two of his early life as a police cadet in Liverpool. When we worked together, it came to be understood by the pupils in the school that he had been a most successful detective inspector who had almost unaided arrested the whole of the Merseyside branch of the mafia. The spread of this belief had a most chastening effect upon those young ladies and gentlemen who regarded education as an unnecessary diversion from the important business of spreading aggravation.

The Pathfinder

If the archaeologist places his confidence in the past, it is the pathfinder who sees new methods and approaches as the key to success in the classroom. He believes that children should be encouraged to write creatively without being inhibited by such peripheral considerations as correct spelling and punctuation. His heart is given to modern mathematics and he is quite happy if children use electronic calculators to make up for their inability to multiply two numbers together. His classroom is arranged with the desks grouped together here and there, and he would no more consider lining them all up and addressing his pupils from the front than expect the children to work in silence. He rarely uses the blackboard, preferring an overhead projector. Unlike some of his colleagues, he does not make a fuss if children fail to call him sir. He has a very close relationship with the sixth form and drinks with them at the local. They call him Dave, and he regards that as a very good sign. He is aware that the headmaster has mixed feelings about him, but has noticed that his classroom is always the one visited when Americans and inspectors of progressive disposition come to the school. He strongly suspects that the chairman of governors, whose conception of education derives from the palaeolithic period, is unaware of his existence.

Generally speaking, Mr St John had a higher opinion of his pupils than his colleagues. He regarded those in the staffroom over forty as educational Bourbons living in the past – a block of old chips overdue for the glad goodbye. The most remarkable thing about him was his absolute confidence in his own approach to teaching, which made him very effective indeed in the classroom. It has been said before in this book, and bears repeating, that the successful teacher is not one who uses this or that method, but one who believes in the approach he employs. Perhaps that point needs taking further. To an extent, an individual's personality bears upon the teaching style he adopts. It would be hard to imagine Mr St John being other than a pathfinder, however long he teaches. Doubtless he will become a shade more conservative in due course, not least because some of his approaches are destined to become the norm, but he is unlikely ever to become a reactionary. His personality shouts: 'Forward!'

The Stickler

This type of teacher concentrates a huge amount of attention on seeing to it that everything is in its proper place. The drawing of margins in exercise books exactly the right distance from the edge of the page is a matter of monumental significance to sticklers; so is the entering of the date at the top of each piece of work in a special manner and position; so is the underlining of headings. Similarly, the chalk has an accustomed location and must always be found there if the stickler's temper is not to come unstuck. Visual aids and classroom notices must always be affixed with four drawing pins, one in each corner. The sight of something hanging by just one or two pins cannot be borne by your genuine, one-hundred-percent stickler. The window sill is another place where sticklerism is applied, each flower and plant having its allotted place in sun or shade, according to its needs. And, just as everything has its particular territory, so does every person. Woe betide the child who exchanges seats with another in the stickler's domain.

Sticklers are more common in the primary than the secondary sector, for two reasons. Firstly, it is easier to stickle in a classroom where one teaches the same children most of the time. Sticklerules are not as easy to apply to a constantly changing clientele as to a relatively fixed one. Secondly, small children are more susceptible to stickling than large ones and perhaps more in need of it. When a child is learning to write, strict and detailed instructions on layout are more important than when he has mastered the skill and is at the stage of writing essays in secondary school.

It is the need for structure that the stickler fastens on as critical to education and there is nothing wrong with that. What young people need is a clear framework within which to operate and the stickler provides just that. For lack of it, children are left drifting on life's ocean without rudder or compass. The fashionable notion that boys and girls must not be subject to discipline but left without constraints to explore the frontiers of human experience is a betrayal of the natural responsibility that falls to adults. A teacher who has not something of the stickler within is not a fit member of the profession.

On the other hand, stickling can become an obsession. Since the beginning of time, mankind has been inclined to invent rules and then to worship them for their own sake after their purpose has been served. Miss Peddie would never allow pupils to use ballpoint pens, arguing that they were messy things that ruined the handwriting. Only after numerous complaints from parents and advice from colleagues was she persuaded that what had been true thirty years before when she entered teaching no longer applied in the late seventies.

Stickling usually reaches its most advanced form in the area of school uniform. The requirement that pupils shall dress in a particular manner for school has consumed the time and energies of teachers and parents to what many see as an unnecessary degree. There is a common complaint from parents that goes something like: 'Teachers should spend their time educating children, not worrying about what they wear.' Interestingly enough, the sort of person who utters it usually has a youngster who is a problem both at home and at school. Lorraine disrupted the few classes she attended in between bouts of truancy. A regular attender at the local juvenile court, she had easily established ascendancy over her young social worker, who admitted being afraid of her. She dressed for school as for a Saturday night session at one of the more seedy local disco joints, that being one more way of making a rude sign at the rest of the world.

Children who make problems over school uniform and get away with it rarely stop there. Some parents and quite a few teachers do not realise how important it is to win the first skirmish when the blast of behavioural battle sounds in the ears. School uniform provides a useful ground upon which to establish the teacher's ascendancy over a pupil disposed to be a troublemaker. Appeasement at that stage is an invitation to the disruptive juvenile to increase his territorial demands. That is not to justify superstickling in the area of school uniform. What it does mean is that a school is best advised to settle upon dress regulations that are reasonable, defensible and capable of being rigidly applied.

My analysis of pedagogic styles is not meant to be exhaustive and there may be teachers who will not recognise themselves in any of the five descriptions given. However, my suspicion is that most will discover themselves somewhere there or, perhaps more likely, be discovered by the colleagues they work with.

But I am oversimplifying matters, and must admit it. In my experience, the average schoolmaster or schoolmistress adopts not one but several styles, using a different methodology with different groups of pupils. It is usually wise to play the stickler with a class in the early stages of a relationship, but a trace of the pathfinder may be allowed to emerge later. A surprising number of teachers manage to look heroic from time to time, school journeys providing an especially good opportunity for that. Mr Munro's feats on Skiddaw amazed his boys, who clearly thought him incapable of peeling an orange without pulling a muscle. Archaeological tendencies develop in most teachers sooner or later, as do inclinations to play the undertaker.

It perhaps needs to be said in conclusion that a teacher's personal qualities and values are not submerged by the pedagogic role adopted in any particular set of circumstances. Whatever performance one presents in the classroom, children will readily perceive the face behind the greasepaint, the person behind the style.

In the preface to this book there is a reference to Walter Bagehot's famous assertion that a teacher should conduct himself 'as if he was amazed at being himself'. That statement conveys a sense of the great responsibilities resting upon a teacher; of the astonishing fact that it should be thought possible for ordinary people to bear them; of the realisation that it can only be done if one steps beyond one's ordinary self and plays a part.

Eight

Salary Negotiations

Voltaire observed that if God did not exist it would be necessary to invent him. If the present arrangements for negotiating the salaries of teachers in England and Wales did not exist, no one would dare to design them for fear of being certified insane or locked up for attempting to undermine the welfare of the nation. They provide a clear example of what Ralf Dahrendorf described as the adversary style of conducting affairs, which he sees as lying at the heart of the nation's economic and associated problems.

In his book *On Britain,* he argues that there has been in this country a notable absence of any 'systematic attempt to create institutions of co-operation'. He continues:

> The prevailing view is that there are irreconcilable conflicts of interest between employers and labour, and that it would be blurring the lines if an attempt was made to share responsibility and authority. Blurring the lines is regarded by both sides as not only inappropriate, but disadvantageous; it restricts the chances of management to give instructions, and the chances of labour to fight all-out battles.

That view is illustrated in the clearest possible way by the structure and activities of the Burnham Committee. The document containing the names of its members sets them out so that the twenty-seven people who make up the management panel and the thirty-two who constitute the teachers' panel are juxtaposed to face one another from different sides of a page, for all the world like two teams in a football programme. Seating at meetings is similarly adversarial, the two sides (a word commonly used to refer to the panels) positioning themselves down the opposite walls of a large room. Invariably, some people have to sit with their backs to those they are supposed to be negotiating with. The chairman is so frequently inaudible that it is something of a joke. When a meeting opens with a complaint from the far end of the room that some people cannot hear what is going on, he good-humouredly asserts, like a scoutmaster addressing his troop, 'I will do my best if everyone else does his best.' As a result of a convention whereby only the teachers' leader and the local authorities' leader may speak in the full committee, it is like nothing so much as a parliament of zombies. This does nothing to generate a feeling that a group of responsible adults with a common interest are involved in rational discussion.

Combative attitudes go along with these arrangements. Anyone on the teachers' panel who shows the slightest disposition to take account of what the local education authorities have to say is immediately howled down as if he were recommending the surrender of the world to invading forces from Mars. When the Professional Association of Teachers was given its Burnham seat at the outset of the 1981 negotiations, the other unions proposed a 15 percent salary claim in response to a 4 percent offer. My suggestion that a more moderate claim be made, lest jobs be placed at risk and students in training faced with zero employment prospects, was greeted with a mixture of incredulity and derision. 'We note the arrival of the PAT on Burnham', said a spokesman for one of the other unions, 'but we believe they should have been put on the management side.' (*Education,* 23 January 1981)

In the event, the 1981 negotiations resulted in a 7½ percent settlement. That figure, acceptance of which was first proposed by me during the course of proceedings, and later by the National Union of Teachers, made nonsense of the opening postures adopted by the two sides. The local education authorities had asserted that money could not be found to pay more than 4 percent; the teachers had declared that a settlement below 15 percent would so demoralise the profession as to bring the education system to a halt. There were, it seemed, lies, damned lies and salary negotiations.

My principal reaction to what happened in 1981 was heaviness of heart at everyone's opening assumption that no identity of interest whatsoever could be acknowledged as existing between the two panels of the Burnham Committee. It was a premise out of touch with common sense. When two children refuse to consider one another's point of view, their teachers tell them not to be silly and immature. Sadly, those who represent the profession in salary negotiations seem unable to live up to the standard of behaviour teachers demand of the young. My answer to media inquiries about how I felt after my Burnham baptism received wide publicity: 'There must be a better way for mature adults to conduct their affairs.'

As fresh negotiations got under way early in 1982, the adversary style was again quickly established when a 12 percent claim brought a 3.4 percent offer by way of a response. In a pre-meeting exchange on 3 March, the leader of one union made his wishes abundantly clear: 'I would like some good grievance to go away with this afternoon.' He got it when the management side declined to agree to a referral to arbitration on the grounds that there had not yet been any negotiating. Disruption of the education system followed with such alacrity that it was obvious plans had been laid to that end in advance.

As the Burnham Committee gathered at Church House Westminster on 25 March to try and sort out the chaos, the NAS/UWT threatened to bring the public examination system to a halt if arbitration was not forthcoming. In fact, at the end of what the chairman described as 'a very long and in some ways strange day', there might have been a settlement at 5.9 percent, but the figure was vetoed by the Department of Education and Science representatives on the management panel, thereby demonstrating that those speaking for the government were no more interested in resolving matters by sensible give and take than the rest of the Burnham Committee seemed to be for most of the time. This fact did not escape the attention of the arbitrators who were now brought in. Their verdict called a plague upon both management and teachers' houses. A 6 percent award in June brought with it a biting observation: 'In the negotiating round of which this arbitration is the final stage, we have been struck by the absence of any sustained serious collective bargaining by the parties.' A straightforward piece of advice was added: 'We recommend that the parties make a serious joint effort to review their procedures.'

The inability of the two sides to act upon such advice was soon demonstrated. On 19 July, a special meeting of the Burnham Committee was called at the request of the teachers' panel to discuss the London allowance. It quickly degenerated into farce. In his opening statement, the leader of the management panel set the tone for the occasion: 'I think, Chairman, it is singularly unfortunate timing that this meeting is being held today.' He found it impossible to make any sort of offer and asked for an adjournment until the autumn. There followed an argument about whether to meet again in September or October. 'There really is no point', observed the management side, 'in carrying on this conversation.' The discussion was 'just becoming silly'. The teachers' leader wasn't having that: 'I do not think it is becoming silly.' The chairman expressed his own particular anxiety: 'Are you leaving the unfortunate decision to me?' That was indeed how it turned out and he settled on a date in the middle of October, the management panel giving an assurance that it would then 'make a serious attempt at a fairly quick resolution'.

As the leaves fell from the trees and the Burnham Committee once more assembled, the promised quick resolution of the London allowance was swept away like so much autumn rubbish. What had looked in July to be a genuine assurance had served its purpose and was now deposited on the dump of discarded management undertakings. The mediators who had been called in to deal with the main 1982 claim, and the 1981 London allowance award before that, were invited to perform an arbitral hat-trick. In consequence, the London allowance for 1982 was not determined until the end of January 1983, by which time a new set of negotiations was imminent.

The events of 1981 and 1982 depict a couple of fairly typical turns of the Burnham carousel. The fact that it never stops going round makes it difficult to service the machinery; the possibility of replacing the equipment with something that gives a reasonably smooth ride is almost non-existent. However, the need for that to be done was drawn to the attention of the Secretary of State for Education and Science as 1982 drew to a close. The response my letter on this subject evoked was significant not because it held out any hope of change, but for what it revealed of how the Minister thought the Burnham machinery should work. He clearly saw its primary function as being not so much the settlement of fair salaries for teachers as the implementation of government economic policy:

> Burnham's record in reaching negotiated settlements is perhaps disappointing, but there are important reasons for that which are not related to its structure – the Government's commitment to economic regeneration and control of inflation expressed in public expenditure policies which deliberately constrain employers' ability to pay, differences of view – even rivalries – between major groupings within one or other panel, and, to be frank, quite unrealistic aspirations amongst some teacher associations. However, whatever view one takes of such current impediments to successful negotiation, the case for review has to be considered on its merits. As you will know, my predecessor and I have both given considerable thought to the arguments for structural change, over quite a period. There emerged no agreement between the parties as to what might replace Burnham, nor do I regard the alleged benefits of change as self-evidently helpful to education. More pragmatically, there is no possibility of legislative time for an amendment to the Act during the present Parliament. I must therefore say plainly to you that I have no plans to re-open the question of changing the present arrangements.

Tucked away in the first part of the opening sentence of that statement is an astonishing assumption. Whatever negotiating machinery exists, one should not expect it to work unless the economic conditions are favourable. Settlement of teachers' salaries by negotiation is not to be expected at a time of expenditure restraint.

It is, of course, arguable that the whole purpose of erecting a complicated negotiating structure is to make agreement possible and likely when conditions are difficult. But the assumption described is the inevitable outcome of belief in the adversary style in industrial relations. It rests upon the conviction that negotiators are out to get the better of one another. Bargaining becomes what Ralf Dharendorf calls a zero-sum game in which one side loses what the other side gains. 'Thoughts of compromise', he writes, 'are not very high in people's minds. One fights to win.' That explains why the arbitrators have been kept so busy in the Burnham context in recent years. The giving of any salary rise at all to teachers has been regarded by management representatives as something to be avoided as long as possible. On the other hand, teachers' representatives have seen their task as being to wring the maximum amount of money out of local education authorities without regard to the economic consequences at local or national level. During the negotiating process, any effective argument advanced by one side is consigned to the goals against column on the other side's scorecard.

It is not inscribed in the heavens that human relations may only be conducted in this way, whether in the field of wage-bargaining or any of the other areas where agreement between one man and another is necessary if civilisation is to survive and flourish. Change is not beyond the bounds of possibility.

What bedevils teachers' salary negotiations at present are the high claim/low offer postures adopted at the outset. Events in 1982 provide an illustration of almost precise mathematical dimensions. The 12 percent opening gambit of the claimants, set against a government norm of 4 percent and an actual offer of 3.4 percent, brought an arbitral award of 6 percent. The relationship between the first two figures and the last speaks for itself. Teachers got half what they had claimed and local education authorities shelled out half again what the government had said was available. Such a simplistic approach to the arbitral process suggests that 3C might have been brought in to carry it out rather than three mighty wizards fetched by ACAS from the land of salary spells and money magic.

There was, of course, never any genuine prospect of a *negotiated* settlement once 3.4 percent had been set against 12 percent, since the two parties involved were so far apart as to be out of sight of one another. The situation was akin to two people attempting to conduct a conversation by shouting from different sides of the Atlantic Ocean. They were so positioned because of the practice whereby arbitrators as often as not settle upon a point about midway between claim and offer. It is that which brings about the high claim/low offer approach.

The problem is exacerbated by another feature of arbitral practice where the last stated positions of the two sides are taken as those to be reconciled. If there is a likelihood that negotiations will be referred to a mediator, all the important exchanges have to be conducted behind the chair, both sides being reluctant to make any kind of concession openly in the Burnham Committee for fear that the whistle will be blown while they are out of position. For example, if an offer of 4 percent is unsuccessfully raised to 5 percent, the arbitral body takes the higher figure as the one representing the management position. Similarly, if the teachers' side unsuccessfully reduces a claim of 15 percent to 12 percent, it is the reduced figure which is taken to be the teachers' position by the arbitrators. As a consequence of this practice, neither panel of the Burnham Committee will significantly change its position in open forum unless it knows in advance that a settlement will automatically follow. Such negotiations as take place are therefore conducted between the leaders of the two panels and their assistants while safely closeted away from the full statutory bargaining body, not to mention over-inquisitive members of their own panels. It is a matter of fact that few members of the Burnham Committee have any first-hand knowledge of what is said or left unsaid in the process of the negotiations to which they are supposed to be party. The disappointed faces of practising teachers appointed to Burnham after years of waiting for seats in this great chamber of debate speak volumes.

When Liverpool decided to abandon the cane, it sent some of its teachers off on a six-week course at the Birmingham University Centre for Child Study. A spokesman for that institution declared that abolition of corporal punishment made it necessary to 'up-skill those working in schools'. (*The Times*, 1 February 1983)

Up-skilling is similarly necessary among teachers' salary negotiators if they are ever to abandon the ritual of beating one another over the head with ineffective utterances. To assist, it is essential that the framework within which they address one another be changed so that, should negotiations break down, arbitrators have but one choice, *viz* to settle either upon claim or offer.

What would be the result of such a change in the arbitral rules? It would compel both sides in negotiations to take up reasonable positions at the outset – a development that would be roughly equivalent to Members of Parliament having to behave themselves at Question Time. Any salary demand out of line with common sense, and known in advance by all concerned to be well beyond available resources, would be self-defeating. Similarly, ludicrously low offers such as those made in recent years would disappear since arbitrators would settle on any reasonable claim made in response. The whole high claim/low offer methodology in salary negotiations would be abandoned.

Single-option arbitration has been advocated by the Professional Association of Teachers in the Burnham Teachers' Panel and at the Department of Education and Science. The fact that it has been treated dismissively in both places is unarguable evidence that it has a great deal to commend it. Support was given to its introduction in the public sector by *The Economist* after the 1982 water strike on the grounds that it would have the effect of 'discouraging both underoffers and overclaims'. Resort to arbitration would become unnecessary since offers and claims would be sufficiently close to one another to make negotiated settlements the order of the day.

But likelihood of such a simple change being brought about is slight, for two reasons. Firstly, it would drastically reduce the power and influence of the two largest teachers' unions, whose public relations policies depend heavily upon their representing themselves as the redeemers of a profession fallen captive to cruel local authority and government taskmasters. Secondly, the ability of the government to dictate teachers' salaries through its representatives on the management side of the Burnham Committee would be removed. Such a self-denying ordinance would be the equivalent of a football manager tying his side's ankles together before sending them out to play at Wembley. It is about as likely as mixed-ability teaching at Eton.

One of the main reasons why HMS Burnham so often runs aground is the ability of the DES commodores on board to stop all engines at the first sign of the vessel making headway towards the land of plenty. Perhaps the crew should be changed. Richard Garner had something to say about that in *The Times Educational Supplement* on 4 February 1983. Referring to what he called 'the sham and pretence of the present set-up', he wrote:

> . . . the teachers should be allowed to negotiate directly with their employers and exclude the Department of Education and Science which has two representatives on the management panel and the power to veto any pay offer. It is nonsense to suggest that removing the DES from the Burnham Committee would strip the Government of all power to influence the size of the teachers' pay settlement. What, for heaven's sake, is the rate support grant settlement all about?

Most members of the profession have little idea how the Burnham Committee is constructed and even less of how it operates. They get on with the job of teaching and are happy to leave the settlement of their salaries to those they pay to deal with such things on their behalf. I have to admit that such was my own attitude during my twenty-three years in schools. Teaching is such an absorbing and demanding activity that one has neither the time nor the inclination to follow events in the annual salary war. One is vaguely conscious of Burnham exchanges as they are reported in the press, but they are not properly comprehended. Only when negotiations break down, as they almost invariably do, does one begin to take notice, and then with some reluctance. Called in recent years to embark upon disruptive practices originally devised to counteract the power of inhuman nineteenth-century factory owners, the average teacher has at first crept unwillingly from school and then begun to ask whether such tactics are appropriate for a body of professionals. The prevailing mood among the majority of teachers in the eighties is that of being caught within a system that does not allow them to act professionally. Many are not sure how it came to be so. They remind one of John Arden's lines:

> Who can tell how the lobster got
> Into the lobster pot?
> When he went in he did not doubt
> There was a passage out.
> There was not.

But it would be misleading to end this chapter on that pessimistic note. The damaging effects upon the image of the profession brought about by teachers behaving like educational factory hands have become increasingly clear in the last two or three years. Fewer teachers than before are now prepared to adopt the ours-not-to-reason-why approach to demands that they bring education to a halt. They have come to realise that industrial action is subject to the Law of Inevitable Escalation, whereby the amount of disruption necessary in pursuit of a given end increases year by year. They have also come to appreciate that one of the reasons for disruption in recent years has been the nature of the negotiating machinery. Most teachers are anxious for ways to be found of pressing the case for adequate funding of education without recourse to activities damaging to children.

In his book *If This Is a Man,* in which he records his experiences at Auschwitz, Primo Levi describes the unquestioning majority of the inmates of that prison camp as the musselmans or drowned ones. They went along with the system and failed to find a way of circumventing 'the infernal knot of laws and prohibitions'. They accepted things as they were and the inevitability of their fate: 'All the musselmans who finished in the gas chambers have the same story, or more exactly, have no story; they followed the slope down to the bottom, like streams that run down to the sea.' The infernal knot that binds the Burnham Committee must be cut if the vision of a genuine profession is not to run down to the sea and be lost in the expanding ocean of a second-rate education service.

Nine

The Future of the
Teaching Profession

I was once taking part in a phone-in radio programme on comprehensive schools when an ex-pupil suddenly came on the line and
made the most astonishing accusations. Trapped within a pair of
earphones, a paper cup containing the most awful coffee ever made
in the history of the world by my elbow, I felt my whole professional
career collapsing around me. What would people think of a man
about whom such things were said? And how could I deal in a few
seconds from a broadcasting studio with charges that I had painted
over naughty pupils' glasses so that they could not see to cause
trouble and shut miscreants inside a dustbin kept in my classroom
for that purpose? On reflection afterwards, I asked myself how I
could have overlooked such excellent disciplinary methods, but at
the time I was nonplussed.

But deliverance was close at hand. Across the airwaves came the
cheerful voice of one of my admirers. 'Hullo, sir', it said, 'it's me,
Jeremy.' As the strains of the *Hallelujah Chorus* sounded in my
subconscious, this splendid young man paid testimony to my gifts
in terms that made Shakespeare's magnificent tribute in *Richard II* to
this teeming womb of royal kings that we call England sound quite
half-hearted.

Since one of the most significant developments in education in
recent years has been the encouragement of teachers to take account
of the opinions of their pupils, it is perhaps no wonder that many of
us are confused. But it is not only boys and girls to whom the
practitioner in the classroom is expected to listen. The ever-growing
army of advisers includes parents, politicians, administrators,
academics, researchers and all kinds of committees and pressure

123

groups. Falling rolls have been matched by rising opinions. Such is the plethora of initialled organisations operating in the field of education that one quickly becomes lost in the world of ACE, CASE, CSSAS, NAGM and ACSET, not to mention STOPP and START. Which voices should one believe? Some teachers overcome this problem by listening to none of them and resting entirely upon their own judgement. The trouble with that is obvious. President John F. Kennedy once observed that the most dangerous moment for a politician is when he starts to believe his own propaganda. It is true also of teachers that, once hermetically encapsulated within their own conception of themselves and their profession, they are ready for launching into educational outer space. But the future of education does not lie out there among the stars. Teaching is a down-to-earth activity. Any realistic assessment of what is to come must relate what is being said and done about education by the various interested parties to what the effect will be upon the child carving his initials on the desk or, more likely these days, writing them in felt-tip pen.

It is without doubt indicative of the way things have been going for many years that calling anyone of secondary-school age a child is no longer acceptable or general practice in some quarters. It is significant that the organisation dedicated to advancing pupil influence calls itself the National Union of School Students (NUSS). The economic advance in the sixties and seventies of the teenager, and then of the sub-teenager, has been an important factor in the social enfranchisement of young people. Together with other important influences mentioned in chapter four, the ability of young people to put their hands in their own pockets and exert effective pressure upon the economic system to provide what they want has changed their relationship with shopkeepers, advertisers, entertainment proprietors, clothes manufacturers and many others who market goods and services. As debate about education has been increasingly conducted in marketing terms, teachers have been depicted as purveyors of a service in a competitive situation. School pupils are customers whose demands must be adequately satisfied. The relationship between teacher and taught is that of producer and consumer.

In order to appreciate the magnitude of the transformation which has taken place since the middle of this century, it is necessary to look back on the relationship between schoolmasters and children that once applied. I call to mind a frequent utterance of the PE master at the school where my teaching career began. 'You are not expected to *like* it', he would say to any boy lacking his own enthusiasm for gymnastics, 'you are expected to *do* it.' In today's world, pupils as often as not choose what they will and will not do by way of physical activity. After the middle-school years, they are often allowed to opt out altogether.

The same right of choice prevails in the classroom from an early age. In some primary schools, children spend as much time deciding which activity or project to pursue as they do carrying it out. An enormous amount of effort is given over during the third year of secondary education to helping pupils decide which subjects to study for examinations in the fourth and fifth. Many secondaries mount spectacular exhibitions of work depicting the options available, for all the world like those run by commercial firms displaying their wares. Schools have come to be more and more like supermarkets. Consumerism rules.

A parallel development is present in the area of discipline. It is not uncommon to find teachers drawing up contracts with recalcitrant pupils in order to persuade them to behave themselves. This approach to discipline has taken a particularly strong hold in intermediate treatment centres and similar institutions, but it has also been adopted by many schools. Based on a particular theory known as behaviour modification, it is perhaps the clearest example of marketing techniques operating in education. It has developed at least in part because those dealing with extremely difficult boys and girls have lost confidence in punishment as a means of correction. An agreement is reached between teacher and pupil listing desirable forms of behaviour and the various rewards attaching to each. This agreement is signed by both parties, the pupil thereby giving an undertaking to strive for the rewards available. Discipline becomes a matter of bargaining. Trading across the table replaces bending over a chair.

Has the right of pupils to choose what they will study and to enter contractual arrangements about their behaviour come to stay? The likelihood is that both will become strongly established features of the education system in the future. The most powerful argument in favour of allowing that to happen is that successful education depends upon motivation. Give a youngster a good enough reason to learn something or behave himself and he will usually do so. The days are in any case past when schools could dictate to children which subjects they might take for public examinations. The reimposition of rigid option patterns would be impossible in most comprehensives. As to behavioural matters, the contractual approach would seem to be the only way ahead as punishment in all its forms is made either illegal or impractical.

To an extent, the argument about corporal punishment which has raged with increasing ferocity in recent years has obscured a more profound issue. Recourse by parents to the European Court of Human Rights to establish that they may decline to have their children punished in that particular way is merely symptomatic of a general movement among parents to decide how their offspring may and may not be treated in school when they have misbehaved. In the last two decades, teachers have come under increasing pressure from those who oppose the practice of detention, dislike the imposition of extra work, remonstrate when constraints are placed on disruptives leaving school premises in the lunch hour, dissent when head teachers confiscate the bus passes of those who make the lives of other travellers a misery and find grounds to oppose each and every sanction introduced to make naughty boys and girls toe the line. There is now a significant and increasing body of parents who are against all forms of punishment. While there have always been some like that, there has been a fundamental change in the situation since the sixties. Firstly, the lengths to which such parents are prepared to go to protect their children's right to be disruptive without fear of any consequences has increased dramatically. Secondly, local politicians and administrators have added their weight to the attack on punitive sanctions of all kinds. The advice generally available from the local education office when a head teacher is challenged is to give way. The appeasement of parents is a first priority in the bureaucratic mind.

Given that it is so, it is not hard to see what the future holds. The signs are that schools will increasingly resort to making bargains with parents or their offspring or both, setting down on paper the precise terms by which this or that boy or girl may remain in school and receive an education, the sanction of suspension being implemented if the contract is broken. This development has in fact already begun. It is not without significance that those who are anxious to trammel the power of teachers in general and head teachers in particular have mounted an attack on the practice of suspension. If that ultimate sanction can be removed, or made so difficult to use as to render resort to it impracticable, the last enemy of those opposed to all forms of punishment will have been destroyed or so it might seem.

But ve teachers haf vays of making children behave, regardless of which sanctions are permitted and which *verboten*. Whatever is done to diminish the ability of members of the profession to punish those whose chief interest is in bringing the teaching process to a grinding halt not later than three minutes into any lesson, the majority remain effective disciplinarians by the simple exercise of their own personalities and pedagogic skills. The greatest weapon a teacher possesses in the attempt to maintain order in the classroom is the double-barrelled shotgun of adulthood and eloquence. There are plenty of children around to testify to a good teacher's ability to cut a troublemaker down to size with a few well-chosen words. In the end, the essential difference between teacher and taught comes through – the first is an adult and the second is a child. In a classroom where there is an educator of quality, it is with teacher that the power lies.

It follows that classroom teaching of high quality must be properly recognised and rewarded in future. It has for too long been a feature of the profession that some of the best practitioners, as well as some of the worst, are quickly promoted out of the classroom into posts which involve a reduced teaching commitment. She who stays at the chalkface is destined never to lay hands on the crock of gold that lies buried on Salary Scale Mountain. A cynic took me aside to give me some advice early in my teaching career: 'If you want to make money at this lark, never mind about the kids – put in for being in charge of the drawing pins.' The mere mention of a post of special responsibility being available generates more speculation in a school staffroom than the Grand National, the Boat Race and the Cup Final put together. But there is no adequate reason why promotion should rest as entirely as it does upon readiness to assume duties outside the classroom. Logic suggests the best salaries should go to those who make the best contribution to the actual teaching of children day by day. In short, there should be a promotion ladder that simply recognises quality teaching[1].

When the 1981 salary settlement was made, it was agreed that a Burnham Committee working party should be set up to review the whole structure of teachers' salaries. Predictably, it has made little progress, since most of the changes that teachers want would cost the local education authorities a great deal of money. But there is another factor also at work, which has to do with the question under discussion. Among the, submissions to the working party at its inception was a request that some method be devised for rewarding good classroom teaching. It is a highly contentious issue because it would require some arrangement for assessing performance.

If the good teacher is to be promoted simply for being just that, who is to carry out the critical process of identification? Could one contemplate a head teacher going round the staff announcing that Miss Bloggs was going up to scale three for being a first-class teacher, but Miss Higgs was only a scale two performer and Miss Maggs would be lucky if she ever left scale one? What that would do to a head teacher's relationship with his staff leaves little to the imagination, especially if the quality of his own performance was in doubt, which has been known. Might one give the task of assessment to advisers and inspectors? Leaving aside the teaching profession's lack of confidence in a great many of them, their numbers and acquaintance with individual teachers in schools would be entirely inadequate. The third alternative has even less

1   Since these words were written, the issue has been brought to the forefront of educational debate by the Secretary of State. In a speech in Canterbury in July 1983, Sir Keith Joseph said: 'We need a system that will allow the best young teachers to progress more rapidly than the rest. We need a system that will give extra rewards to the mature classroom teacher of exceptional talent, without requiring promotion to posts carrying managerial responsibility.'

appeal, namely giving the job to union representatives. The person at a school most likely to enjoy being given the task of evaluating the staff would be the school keeper. The ex-navy CPO who kept my school during my headship made devastatingly accurate assessments of my colleagues, and doubtless of me as well. But it would be somewhat wide of the mark to say the staff had a deep affection for him.

It would appear that, desirable as promotion on the basis of teaching performance might be, it is made impossible by the difficulty of deciding who should be the judge of merit. There are similar issues that tie our society into knots of the same shape. Many people go along with the idea of euthanasia in principle and can see the need for it, but cannot decide who is suitable to say when a damaged or senile human being has reached the point when he would be better off dead. As the great Dr William Sangster used to say from his Westminster pulpit, it is not the question *whether* that presents life's greatest dilemmas but the question *who* and the question *why*.

Perhaps the body to decide which teachers' classroom performance merits promotion, and on what grounds, would be capable of solution if a General Teaching Council were established. Meanwhile, an individual's movement up the Burnham salary ladder will continue to reflect his movement out of the classroom into the world of such things as pastoral care, curriculum planning, timetable building, departmental leadership, deputy headship and, for a relatively small proportion of teachers, headship. The point is clearly illustrated by the salary scales for the year beginning 1 April 1983 and effective at the time of this book's publication. Anyone who makes it all the way from the bottom of the qualified teachers' scales to the summit of those for head teachers will begin with little more than £5000 a year but end up with something approaching £22,000. However, strait is the gate that gives access to such riches and few there be that enter there. Most of those who go to make up the teaching force of 400,000 souls are at best likely to get three-quarters of the way up the qualified teachers' scales, earning about £10,500 a year at the top of scale three for assuming responsibilities above and beyond simply teaching children. But a teacher who settles for staying in the classroom and assuming no special responsibilities whatever will fall short of £9,000.

Although these figures will change as new Burnham settlements are made, the relationship between them, and the message that relationship conveys, will not vary significantly unless and until a new salary structure emerges. In the current scales, someone who chooses to remain simply a classroom practitioner is at best scheduled for a 69 percent increase in salary between beginning and end of career. By contrast, a teacher who decides to assume special responsibilities is scheduled for a 102 percent increase if good enough to reach scale three, and a further 25 percent if admitted to the promised land beyond, where verdant scale four pastures lie. From there, the first clear glimpses of Headship Hill may be seen through the clouds of promotional uncertainty. The story of the salary scales is clear – he who would highly salaried be must take the path that leads away from the chalkface and press onward and upward to other things.

At the end of August 1962, *The Times Educational Supplement* published an article on how teachers achieved promotion. The top salary for a head teacher at that time was £2,800, or one-eighth of what it is today, and the piece in question charted the path by which a young schoolmaster might reach such dizzy heights. There was even a suggestion that he might perchance venture beyond into educational administration or teacher training where a staggering £3,000 beckoned. 'The perceptive young graduate', said the writer of the piece, 'should ignore old wives' tales dating from the days when all teachers were badly paid and plan the first formative decade of his professional career as carefully as a military campaign.' As a young history master at the time, I happened to be teaching my GCE O level class about the 1889 dock strike and John Burns' vision of wealth for dockers. Speaking on Tower Hill, he looked to the horizon and saw there the bright gleam of 'the full round orb of the dockers' tanner'. Twenty years ago, it seemed to the teaching profession that there was a silver glow on their financial horizon. How to follow what *The Times Educational Supplement* called the high road to affluence was set out in a diagram which, although reflecting a somewhat different educational structure from that of today, amounts to more than an historic relic, since many of its tongue-in-cheek perceptions remain applicable (see overleaf). Summarising the implications of his analysis, the writer had this advice to offer:

> It is important . . . not only to be a good teacher but to appear to have qualities which merit special notice. The young teacher should, therefore, be punctual, well-dressed, deferential to his elders, and willing to do little tasks. In his second appointment he can organise sports days, visits, coaching *et cetera,* and perform onerous duties which tire his elders. He should show spark and initiative yet not tread on too many educational corns. In his third post others will be doing little tasks for him. He should, therefore, commence desultory part-time studies for Dip Ed, MA, MEd, BSc(Econ) in the hope that a fourth appointment will materialise before it becomes necessary to take any exams. The weight of new responsibility will then prevent him completing the course and everyone will applaud his manifest self-sacrifice.

Regarding his diagrammatic presentation of the way to wealth, the writer expressed the hope that it would prove 'as illuminating to those approaching the maypole for the first time' as it would be 'consoling to those entangled inextricably in its braids'. Today, the promotion system continues to lead education a dance. The existence of the Burnham working party on salary structure arises from general recognition of this both among teachers and those who employ them. There is just a shade too much truth in some of the statements contained in the sixties' article which has been quoted; even more disturbing is the fact that the teacher of the eighties recognises them as describing the promotion stakes as he or she knows and experiences them today.

But even if there is to be a fairly long wait before any method of directly rewarding high-quality teaching has been worked out, one important development in the eighties will significantly alter the manner in which promotion is secured, namely the expansion of in-service training for teachers (INSET). There has been an increasing emphasis in this decade on the importance for teachers of continuing their training beyond the point of entry to the profession and that

High Road to Affluence

	A PRIMARY	B SECONDARY MODERN	C SECONDARY GRAMMAR	D COMPREHENSIVE
FIRST	Desire to forgo specialisation. Interest in development of the young child. Importance of the primary stage as firm foundation for later development. Most primary schools will be so short of staff that polished phrases are not even asked for.	Attracted by the freedom of fresh approach of the secondary modern school. Greater scope for ideas and initiative. Concern for the welfare of less able pupils. The historian must be prepared to teach science, mathematics, geography and scripture. The geographer may be offered a timetable of woodwork, music, technical drawing and English.	Belief in the role of the grammar school in providing future managers and scientists and responsible educated citizens. Admiration for the fine tradition and record of the particular school. Wish to contribute to it. Readiness to assist in and out of season with scouts, cadets, foreign travel, rowing, sailing, swimming, rugby, cricket, hockey, tennis, running, jumping, debates, dramatics and the school piggery.	Combination of two preceding columns with emphasis on attachment to the comprehensive principle, the weaknesses of 11 plus, and ending the sense of failure.
SECOND	*From B, C or D.* Claim desire for experience over the whole age range, firm foundation, centres of interest, projects, assignments, &c. Prepare to swallow the dogma that education consists of the theories and techniques propounded by the head. Useful move for F or G or headship.	*From A.* Unwise move unless contemplating F or G. Prepare for shock. *From C.* Claim desire to work with less gifted children and freedom. Useful for F, G or headship. *From D.* Claim concern for less able child and belief that comprehensive approach can be best applied in more personal atmosphere of a small school.	*From A or B.* Claim desire to broaden experience and work with able children. Very difficult move to accomplish. Previous three years not counted as teaching experience. No financial advantage. *From D.* A doubtful move. Claim attachment to conventional virtues of grammar school and disillusionment with size and impersonality of comprehensive. Useful move for F or secondary modern school headship.	*From B.* A wise move. Claim belief in virtues of comprehensiveness, disillusionment with lack of direction in secondary modern and desire to teach wider range of ability. Chance of early head of department if specialising in E.S.N.s. Sop to parity of esteem. *From C.* Claim disillusionment with straitjackets of examinations, lack of scope for enterprise and interest in whole range of ability. Good financial prospects.
THIRD	Too late to move unless to F or G.	*From A.* Disillusionment would be genuine. *From C.* Practice intercommunion of all leading churches.	*From A.* Absolutely impossible move. *From B or D.* Highly unlikely move. No financial prospect. Six years' service counts as two years' teaching experience.	*From A.* Unlikely move unless there is a serious staff shortage. *From B.* No advantage to be gained. *From C.* A good move.
Aim	*Aim.* Change school and apply for deputy headships of large schools rather than headships of small schools. Adopt a favoured charity or sell saving certificates. Study Masonic signs. Technical college will put on appropriate course if more than 10 apply. Pursue large headships. Salary Group VI – £1,980.	*Aim.* Head of department or deputy headships of large schools. Group X. Salary, £1,740. Pursue large headships. Group X – £2,180.	*Aim.* Head of department posts. Grade C salary, £1,785. Join Rotary and/or golf club. Pursue headships. Group XVI. Salary, £2,480.	*Aim.* Heads of department in comprehensive and modern schools. Extol virtues of comprehensives in letter to *Guardian* and *The Times Educational Supplement.* Pursue headships. Group 22. Salary, £2,800.

APPOINTMENT

E TECHNICAL COLLEGES	F ADMINISTRATION	G TRAINING COLLEGES
Most vital feature of modern educational scene. Fresh and stimulating in contrast with the secondary field. Chance to experiment with new ideas and techniques. Acquaintance with selection of symbols, e.g., C.G.L.I., P.T.C., R.S.A., T.T.D.A., day release, sandwich courses, &c., useful here, also practical interest such as sports car specials, miniature liquid fuel rockets. Ingrained dirt due to above can be an added qualification.	Teaching experience required.	Possible, but once installed it is difficult to break out. Better leave it till you have exhausted other fields or they have exhausted you.

APPOINTMENT

E	F	G
Once established, stay here. Whole field expanding rapidly. Good promotion prospects and high salaries. *From A.* Not a feasible move unless you can draw some analogy between the examination requirements of the 11 plus and the Institute of Meat. *From B and D.* Claim that technical college is natural extension to modern/comprehensive school. Chance to follow through the process. Closer links needed. Quote White Paper and appear practical. *From C.* Stress specialist qualification. Claim high standards and good examination results. Claim to have been unsung prophet of techs as routes for abler grammer school pupils. Suggest techs ought to take over all "A" level work from grammar school.	*From A-E.* Try the market but do not despair at negative response. Begin cultivating HMIs, LEA inspectors, administrative types and college contacts.	*From A-E.* Possible, but these are early days to be contemplating retirement.

APPOINTMENT

E	F	G
From A. Unthinkable move. *From B, C and D.* A difficult move but still worthwhile. *Aim.* Climb the ladder, grades A-B, lecturer, head of departments Grades I-VI, e.g., Grade II head of department. Salary, £2,050 plus time off for research. At £2,000 clean finger nails and peddle courses at executive level to industry. Pursue principalships at £2,800.	*From E.* Claim first hand acquaintance with technical college administration. Read White Paper Cmnd. 1254 and Building Bulletin No. 5. Decry regionalisation and stress unity of Education Service. Financially you will probably lose ultimately. *From A-D.* Claim varied and responsible teaching experience and interest and readiness for responsibility over the whole field of education. Praise vitality of primaries, courage of moderns, tradition of grammars, high hopes of comprehensives, dynamic of technical colleges and ideals of enlightened administration. Purchase pipe and bowler. Send wife out teaching and run a "Jag" on car allowance. *Aim.* C.E.O. at £3,000 plus.	*From E.* A gamble which might pay off. Some future Minister is bound to demand training for technical college staffs and you would be one of the first in the field. *From A-D.* Claim varied and responsible experience. Revise your theory, heurism, apperception, Gestalt, &c. Thicken your hide. Everyone will criticise you, only your students will temporarily recognise your authority and no one will heed your research. *Aim.* Principal at £2,800 plus.

(*The Times Educational Supplement*, 31 August 1962)

has been underlined both in the White Paper *Teaching Quality* and in the decision announced by the Secretary of State for Education and Science at Easter 1983 to provide direct grants to local education authorities for designated in-service training courses. The Advisory Committee for the Supply and Education of Teachers (ACSET) has already committed itself to giving close attention to in-service training as an early priority. By the mid-eighties, INSET will be a word as much a part of common educational parlance as ROSLA once was. More to the point, those teachers who keep their distance from it will almost certainly have their prospects of promotion blighted. One of the areas of in-service training to which the scheme for direct financial assistance to local education authorities applies is that of management training for head teachers and other senior school staff. In the Department of Education and Science document setting out the scheme (Circular 3/83), the reason is made clear: 'The Secretary of State sees a pressing need for head teachers and other senior teachers carrying out management functions to be better equipped for their increasingly difficult and complicated tasks.'

Many of the influences that have made school management increasingly difficult and complicated in recent years have also made the task of the ordinary classroom teacher both more demanding and more hazardous than before. Leaving aside the question of initial and in-service training, are there any ways in which the young school-master or schoolmistress of the eighties is being equipped to deal with this? The majority of those now entering the maintained sector of education as teachers have three characteristics which were less general in the past. They are destined to become almost invariable in the not-too-distant future.

The first characteristic of the pedagogue of the eighties is that he has been educated in a comprehensive school. The process by which the teaching profession has been transformed into a body of people each of whom is properly equipped to understand all sorts and conditions of young people has, of course, been going on for a long time. But there remains a residue of practitioners whose experience both as pupils and teachers has been mainly in the selective framework, so the transformation is not yet complete. The view therefore still prevails in some dark corners of the profession that, when God created heaven and earth and all that therein is, he made some children different in value from others. Of course, it is fiercely denied that such attitudes prevail, but the allocation of resources to different kinds of school under the old tripartite system gave the game away. Even today, there is a tendency for teachers of those who find learning difficult to be held in less esteem and to have poorer prospects of promotion than those working with what are sometimes called academic pupils. We are still a decade or two away from treating all children as if they matter equally. But the profession advances towards that green and pleasant land.

The second characteristic of the teacher of today and the future is that he or she has entered the classroom from choice rather than by default. This is a feature to which reference has already been made in chapter three. In the sixties and seventies, and before that, sixth-formers frequently trained as teachers because they were not up to university entrance standard. Taking up teaching was a generally recognised way of staying in the education system if you were not sure what else to do and had rather liked school. It was seen as a particularly good way for a young woman to occupy herself prior to matrimony and had the added attraction that she would be able to go on doing it afterwards without serious risk of being identified as a career woman who put her work before her husband. Not so a young woman who became a solicitor, chartered accountant or department store manageress; she bore the unmistakable signs of the careerist. Even if it were not so, entering teaching by default has declined dramatically as a result of training institutions raising their entry requirements and the contraction of employment opportunities. By the time the tide turns later in the eighties, when we will very likely be back into teacher shortages again at primary level, the method-ology of teacher selection will very likely have been tightened up in line with the recommendations of the White Paper *Teaching Quality*, and there might even be a General Teaching Council. The teacher of the future will be someone who has entered the profession as a result of a positive commitment to teaching and a proper assessment of suitability.

The third characteristic of the teacher of today and tomorrow is that he and she will close ranks with colleagues. While the tripartite system of education created a divided profession, comprehensivi-sation brings its members closer together. The disposition of teachers of French and physics and high flyers to look down on their colleagues who teach engineering and housecraft and children with least ability is in decline. The heads of departments meeting in a comprehensive school has proved to be a teacher-training medium of great significance. In the cut and thrust of debate about the curriculum, allocation of resources, public examination entries and all the rest of the heartbreakingly insoluble issues facing a school in deciding its priorities, Mr Duggan was slowly but surely made to think again about questions which had not disturbed his mind for twenty years, it being finely tuned to the exclusive needs of GCE chemistry candidates. 'Look', said he, 'there's no point in spending money on books for these young ones who can't read when my examination groups haven't any balances.' Mr Duggan always referred to first-formers as 'these young ones'. He once expressed the view that serious teaching did not begin until the age of thirteen. Everything that came earlier was seen in the same category as playing with bricks and sand. But the head of the remedial department provided an unanswerable response to his preference for balances over books. There was in Mr Duggan's sixth-form class at that time a brilliant young man who was being lined up for an Oxbridge place. The whole staff had listened to Mr Duggan's repeated predictions about the likely academic achievements of John Brightside. They were expressed in such terms as to make clear where the credit for them would exclusively lie. 'I wonder', said the head of the remedial department, 'if Mr Duggan is aware that John Brightside was in my department for his first two years in this school?' The recipient's astonished reaction to this piece of infor-mation was the same as the one he gave on discovering from a colleague that a woman had been appointed head of mathematics: 'Good God, you don't say!'

There are forces at work to delay the closing of teachers' ranks. Government policies on education are inhibiting the establishment of genuine comprehensive schools. The assisted places scheme provides one example; measures to re-establish technical schools provide another. How long these and other preservatives will cause division to survive, and to what extent, remains to be seen. They will in any case not prevent the comprehensivisation of the greater part of the maintained education system from having its effect. The teaching profession will never be as divided in the future as it was in the past.

That is not to say that teachers will cease to argue with one another. The multiplicity of unions among them is exactly what one would expect of a profession in which taking a different point of view from one's colleague is a matter of pride. However strong the case for doing this, there will always be someone standing ready to argue the case for doing that. In the *Education Year Book* there are listed over five hundred organisations catering for different activities and interest groups among educators.

But there is one thing that few teachers would disagree about as 1984 approaches, namely the need to restore the image of the profession. In the summer of 1975, *The Times* diarist one day devoted his column to some books for schools specially written to reflect situations with which young people were familiar. In one of them, the hero (*sic*) was a teenager suspended for pushing his teacher over.

Pushing teachers about has, figuratively speaking, become something of a national pastime in the last couple of decades. In the opening passages of this book I referred to the readiness of the adult population to pass judgement on them. Some of the judgements that have been made have seriously damaged the image of the teacher.

If the teaching profession is to retrieve the high regard of parents and justify its claim to be an institution of consequence, a great deal needs to be done. In the preceding chapters, I have dealt with the principal issues bearing upon the future condition of those who practise the art and science of teaching. It remains for me to summarise the main steps by which genuine professionalism may be established among teachers.

Too many words have been written in one quarter or another about the meaning of the word professional for me to feel disposed to add significantly to them, especially as I have no academic creden-

to bring to this complex sociological concept. But there are four
*e*ments which seem to me to have obvious relevance to the position
of the teacher.

Firstly, a professional possesses a *skill* not generally available to
all. A good teacher has a particular innate ability that cannot be
acquired. To describe the teacher's skill is not easy, but it is
immediately recognisable in those who possess it. It has something
to do with a natural mastery of communication. To see the very best
teachers at work, one would think they had somehow managed to
climb inside their pupils' minds. Not all the training in the world
can provide someone with this ability. A close parallel is provided in
the world of sport. It is sheer agony for someone with no ability at
handling a ball to be made to play ball games. Conversely, those
with a natural talent need little or no training in order to perform
with considerable proficiency. To an extent, both teachers and
tennis players are born, not made. There is plenty of evidence that,
just as some people with no talent for the game are thrust on to the
tennis court, so some unfortunate individuals take up the craft of the
classroom by mistake. The fact that they remain there is of little
benefit to anyone, least of all themselves. It is a serious act of
negligence on the part of the profession that it has not bestirred
itself to do something about them.

Secondly, a professional has undergone a particular form of
training before being admitted to the community of practitioners.
There is no inconsistency between this point and the first. Although
a college course cannot make a teacher out of someone who has not
got what it takes, an adequate system of teacher education performs
a number of functions. One of these is to sharpen and direct the
skills trainees possess; another is to provide them with sufficient
straightforward knowledge in the subjects they are to teach; yet
another is to provide some understanding of the education system
within which they will be working once qualified. Anyone who
enters the profession without proper training is at a disadvantage,
however great their natural talent. Measures to bring to an end the
era of the untrained teacher are to be thoroughly applauded.

Thirdly, a professional belongs to a body of practitioners who
collectively possess *control of entry* to their own ranks. This is one of

the two areas in which teachers still appear to be a very long way from achieving genuine professional status.

Fourthly, a professional has a *particular attitude towards responsibilities*. He or she works until a task is properly completed rather than within fixed hours; is keenly interested in the quality of the service being offered; makes a uniquely personal contribution to whatever overall provision is being made by the professional group. It is not difficult to see how far teachers have drifted away from this fourth aspect of professionalism in recent years. They have not been the only ones. Along with the development of group practices in medicine, there seems to have grown the notion that it is only proper for citizens to be sick at certain times. General practice seems to have become a matter of working to fixed hours and getting through a given quantity of patients rather than offering a unique personal service of high quality. There has developed a corresponding disposition among teachers in the last decade or two, as has already been spelled out earlier in this book. Happily, nothing that unions, politicians or bureaucrats can do will ever be able completely to alter the fact that every teacher in the end decides for himself what sort of service to offer.

The three most important steps necessary to the advance of teachers towards full professionalism follow naturally from what has been said. Firstly, there must be better teacher selection and training. Secondly, there must be a General Teaching Council. Thirdly, there must be a reappraisal of teachers' attitudes towards their responsibilities, both by teachers themselves and the society they serve. The time has come for a more explicit definition than before of what is expected of members of the teaching profession. The proper determination of conditions of service, preferably by negotiation within a statutory body, would be an important contribution to this. Although there are fears that such definition would diminish a teacher's freedom to act as a professional, the opposite might well prove to be the case. Teachers are likely to enjoy greater freedom of action within a properly defined structure than at present, when they wait upon a variety of principalities and powers to tell them what to do and what not to do.

In *The Backbench Diaries of Richard Crossman,* the author offers his candid observations on party political conferences after having attended those of the two major parties in 1956:

> What the Conservative Conference wanted, if you had asked its general will, was to make war on Nasser, restore the cat, smash the trade unions and relieve the middle class of taxation. How odious, you say. But now turn to the Labour Party. Here there is an equal and opposite extremism of emotion. Here the delegates were much more inclined to be pro-Nasser than pro-British and to be fantastically pacifist. The Labour Conference is temperamentally anti-British, anti-war, for giving everything away and for taking everything away from anybody who has anything. This, I must say, is an odious frame of mind.

The polarisation of views which party politics brings about, described so lucidly in that passage by one of parliament's most perceptive analysts, has become a genuine danger in schools. Media coverage of education sometimes gives the impression that teachers can be neatly divided into floggers and strokers; those who are nice to children and those who are nasty to them; those who are concerned about academic standards and those wanting to bring in the revolution; those in favour of selection and those implacably opposed to it; those who support their head teachers and those who work to undermine their authority; those who wear scruffy jeans and sniff glue in front of their classes and those who conduct themselves in a traditional manner. But it is not so. Most teachers are found at neither extreme of the spectrum of educational opinion and practice. They are preoccupied with their own classes and their own pupils and often unaware of the significance of much that is being said about them or done in their name. For example, most classroom practitioners have never seen the Burgundy Book describing their conditions of service, could not accurately name the seven unions which sit on the Burnham Committee and would have difficulty in finding the Department of Education and Science.

For ordinary teachers, ignorance of these things brings its own special kind of bliss. Most concentrate their interest on their pupils and find their satisfaction within the four walls of the classroom. That is the right professional priority, since it is the style and quality of the individual's performance as an educator that matters most to those who are the customers of the education service. Whatever happens to education between now and the end of the eighties, the preservation of that priority is essential if the value of the teaching profession is to be adequately recognised and its claim to be a profession endorsed by the society it serves.

The future of education therefore rests less upon the grand sweep of political policy than some imagine; less upon the ascendancy of this or that pressure group than some strive for; less upon commitment to particular methods than some believe. For the man or woman in the classroom, the awful and exciting truth is that the future rests right there. Whatever war may be waging over education at Westminster or county hall at three o'clock on a wet Wednesday afternoon, the teacher is captain of his fate and master of his soul in that small rectangle of the educational territory which is his classroom; or if he is not, it is his own fault. Winston Churchill once observed: 'There is nothing in life so exhilarating as to be shot at without result.' The good teacher will always be secure, whatever political or administrative battles rage around the school system, and it is upon the good teacher that the future of education depends.

Appendix One

School Meals Agreement

The existing agreement on what are generally known as dinner duties was drawn up by the Working Party on Teachers and the School Meals Service which was set up by the Secretary of State for Education and Science in December 1967. Its terms of reference were: 'To consider and make recommendations on the position of teachers in relation to all aspects of the School Meals Service.' The working party, which was made up of representatives of the local education authority associations and unions existing at that time, presented its report in the summer of 1968 with an assurance that all accepted the recommendations being made. As a result, the Secretary of State implemented the report in the following terms:

> Having received this assurance from the associations of local education authorities and of teachers of support for the principles set out in the report and of their undertaking to give their fullest support in securing the implementation of the recommendations in the light of these principles, the Secretary of State has amended the Provisions of Milk and Meals Regulations 1945 so as to remove with effect from 16 August 1968 the powers of local education authorities to require teachers to undertake supervision of pupils taking a school meal.

In its preamble, the working party made a number of important statements before coming to the point of making recommendations:

1   We have taken as our principal aim that of finding a way of abolishing the provision in the Regulations which

enables authorities to require teachers to supervise pupils taking school dinners without impairing the school meals service or adding unreasonably to its cost, while continuing to provide adequately for the safety and welfare of the children during the mid-day break.

2 We have reviewed the previous history and present practice of the part played by teachers in connection with the School Meals Service, particularly as regards the supervision of pupils taking school dinners, and also of the part played by supervisory and clerical assistants. We have done so against the background of developments in the schools. We have taken account of what happens in Scotland where teachers are not required to supervise children taking school dinners.

3 Among the more important of the educational and social developments has been the increasing tendency of teachers to engage in voluntary extra-curricular activities between the morning and afternoon sessions and after the school day has finished. This has been accompanied by an increasing tendency for children to spend the mid-day break at school. There have been many reasons for this. There has been the increasing range of extra-curricular activities; the growing number of children both of whose parents are in employment; the closure of small village schools so that more children have to travel further to school; the re-organisation of secondary schools into larger units; and the increase in the number of parents who think it desirable and natural that their children should be provided with a mid-day meal at school, just as they themselves are provided with meals at their place of work.

4 The increasing numbers staying at school at mid-day to take school meals, the development of out-of-school activites, and, in general, the rapid changes in curriculum and organisation have placed greater responsibilities on the schools and their staffs. They have also increased the importance of the role played by the school's catering facilities in the life of the school, both at mid-day and

after school. This is a development which we think should be encouraged. The arrangements made for the provision of school meals have naturally been affected. To alleviate the growing burdens falling on teachers there has been a steady increase in the employment of ancillary helpers to assist in supervising school meals and in other non-teaching tasks, and free school meals have been provided for teachers engaged in the oversight of pupils who stay at school for their mid-day meal.

5   Activities which take place between sessions and after school differ in their nature from those that take place during sessions, since in general the former are voluntary and the latter compulsory. There are differences also between the provision of school dinners, which is required by statute, and other extra-curricular activities, which are not so required. This legal distinction does not, however, mean that any of the activities which take place between sessions and after school are unimportant. They all play a positive part in making the school a 'live' and flourishing educational institution in the interests of the pupils.

6   Clearly the success of these activities depends on the extent and quality of the voluntary efforts of individual teachers under the leadership of the head teacher. The head teacher must retain overall responsibility for the conduct of the school meal, just as he does for all that takes place in and about the school and there is a professional responsibility on the teaching staff as a whole to support the head teacher in fulfilling these responsibilities. It is also important to the teacher, whether head or assistant, that he should be able to enjoy a proper and satisfactory break in which he can relax and rest and, if he wishes, leave the school premises.

These observations were followed by five specific recommendations:

(i)   that Regulation 14 should be amended so as to remove the power given to authorities to require teachers to supervise pupils taking dinners;

(ii) that teachers who undertake the oversight of pupils during the mid-day break should be entitled to have a free school dinner, and other teachers remaining should be able to have their dinner on payment;

(iii) that authorities, after consultations with their teachers, should review their arrangements relating to supervisory assistance in the schools in the light of the principles set out above and in accordance with the suggestions made in the Annexe;

(iv) that authorities, after consultation with their teachers, should review their arrangements relating to clerical assistance in the schools to ensure that teachers are not expected to undertake unreasonable burdens relating to the general administration of the School Meals Service;

(v) that all the bodies represented on the Working Party should undertake to give their fullest support in securing the implementation of these recommendations in the light of the general principles set out in this report.

The working party was aware that, as a result of its recommendations, the School Meals Service would have in future to be staffed to a greater extent than before by paid supervisory assistants. It was recommended that local education authorities should review their arrangements in consultation with teachers, and that 'this consultation should include an opportunity for each school to indicate the number of ancillary helpers that it requires.' There followed an Annexe giving a suggested scale of provision:

Infants
1 ancillary helper for every 30 children remaining at school.

Juniors
1 ancillary helper for every 75 children remaining at school, up to a normal maximum of 4 helpers.

Secondary
1 ancillary helper for every 200 pupils remaining at school, up to a normal maximum of 5.

The working party recognised that the suggested secondary provision would be inadequate in many schools because of varying circumstances. It was extremely difficult 'to indicate a scale for the normal case'.

Appendix Two

Unified Negotiating Machinery

When Mark Carlisle was Secretary of State for Education and Science, he made the first serious attempt to create a single unified negotiating machinery for the pay and conditions of service of teachers in England and Wales. Although unsuccessful, the proposals he put forward in January 1981 have a certain historic significance and are therefore reproduced in full below.

Introduction

1 The Secretary of State is reviewing the Remuneration of Teachers Act 1965 and present arrangements for negotiating teachers' pay and other conditions of service. This Note sets out his aims and intentions for the main features of new negotiating arrangements, for discussion with the teachers' associations. Consultation is proceeding in parallel with the local authority associations.

General Principles

2 The Secretary of State aims:
   (i)   to secure new unified national negotiating arrangements covering all conditions of service including pay (but excluding pensions) for teachers employed at schools and further education institutions maintained by local education authorities in England and Wales, such arrangements to be effective for the 1982 negotiations;
   (ii) to secure that the conditions of service including pay thus determined shall apply to teachers throughout all local education authorities;

(iii) to ensure that the new arrangements are as simple, flexible and economic as possible, consistent with securing the above features and with devising arrangements that are workable and durable.

3 These aims, and the proposals that follow, are based on the Secretary of State's interest in teachers' pay and other conditions of service, deriving directly from his general responsibilities under the Education Acts, from the interaction between resources and the quality and range of educational provision, and from the scale of resources involved nationally.

Structure

4 Two negotiating committees are proposed, one covering teachers in primary and secondary education and one for those in further education. Each committee would consist of a management panel and a teachers' panel under independent chairmanship.

5 The members of the management panels will be the local authority associations (the AMA, the ACC and the WJEC) and representatives of the Secretary of State. Detailed composition and procedures of the panels will be for the local authority associations and the Secretary of State to agree.

6 The Secretary of State is willing to consider suggestions by the teachers' associations as to how the composition of the teachers' panels should be set and varied. Possibilities include determination, as in the present Burnham arrangements, by the Secretary of State; initial determination only by him; determination and variation by the panels themselves, perhaps with recourse to the Secretary of State in the event of major differences arising. The working procedures of the teachers' panels will be for them to decide.

Settlements

7 The intention is that reviews of conditions of service (including pay) could be initiated by the committees themselves or by the Secretary of State. Normally a settlement should be

reached by negotiation, only exceptionally by recourse to arbitration. A settlement once made should be capable of rapid dissemination and implementation, being embodied in documents that are as simple as possible consistent with securing uniform application in England and Wales, continuity of transition from present provisions, and the minimum of appeal for interpretation.

8   The Secretary of State proposes that responsibility for making arbitral arrangements should rest with him, after consultation with the other parties. Arbitration should be a device of last resort and he would want to see arrangements that were conducive to thorough negotiation as the norm for every settlement. To this end he invites views on the proposal that access to arbitration under the proposed new machinery should be voluntary, that is only by the agreement of both panels.

9   The Secretary of State is considering what long stop powers he should seek in respect of a settlement, whether arrived at by negotiation or through arbitration. For arbitral awards he proposes a statutory power to set an award aside and to substitute a different determination by Order subject to annulment by resolution of either House or Parliament. Such a power would be used only exceptionally but some reserve power is regarded as essential because of his overall national responsibilities.

Legislation
10   Legislation will be required to repeal or amend the 1965 Act and possibly for some of the main features of the new arrangements. However the Secretary of State proposes that these should be voluntary rather than statutory, as far as is possible. Matters requiring statutory force might include the national application of settlements, power to make and vary arbitral arrangements, reserve powers in respect of negotiated settlements or arbitral awards, and determination of the composition of the panels. Other matters requiring statutory force may be identified during consultation.

Other Issues

11 Various other aspects will require consideration:

    (i)   the status of the new committees – statutory or non-statutory;

    (ii)   specification of the field to be reviewed; there may be advantage in a non-exclusive definition so as to allow the possibility of admitting kindred groups in the future;

    (iii) transmission of negotiated settlements to the Secretary of State;

    (iv) working procedures for committees and panels – the one-voice convention, etc.;

    (v)   chairman's appointment, role and remuneration;

    (vi) future arrangements for 'Committee of Reference' functions;

    (vii) manpower implications, secretariat arrangements and recording of proceedings.

Conclusion

12 The Secretary of State invites the collaboration of the teachers' associations in the devising and introduction of new unified negotiating machinery; and in particular their views on:

    (i)   structure of the committees, and determination of composition of the teachers' panels (paras 4 and 6);

    (ii)   initiation of reviews, and dissemination and application of agreements (para 7);

    (iii) arbitration arrangements (para 8);

    (iv) reserve powers on arbitral awards (para 9);

    (v)   minimal necessary statutory provision (para 10);

    (vi) other issues (para 11).

Appendix Three

General Teaching Council

The statement which follows is contributed by a member of the Steering Committee of the Campaign for the General Teaching Council (CATEC).

Introduction
Some two years after the creation of the General Medical Council in 1849, a number of prominent teachers, hoping that they could gain for themselves and their profession the kind of esteem that doctors were newly enjoying, began to lobby Parliament for a General Council of their own. They knew that only such a device would allow them to rid their ranks of the incompetent amongst them; they realised that if *teachers themselves* were able to set the admission standards for their own profession, they had a vested interest in seeing that they were high. Now, one hundred and twenty or so years later, after many false starts, several Education Acts and alternate Governmental bouts of encouragement and rejection of the idea, the establishment of a General Teaching Council in England and Wales (Scotland, of course, has possessed one since 1965) seems even further away than it must have seemed then.

Functions
What would a General Teaching Council do? In order to be effective it would have to have the following duties:
1   It would keep a Register of all those qualified to teach; those whose names did not appear on the Register would not be allowed to teach in schools in England and Wales.
2   It would establish a Code of Conduct and a Disciplinary Committee, amongst the sanctions of which would be the power to strike names from the Register.

3   It would admit the names of practitioners to its Register after satisfying itself that the courses that they had followed were suitable and an appropriate probationary period had been served according to its standards.

4   It would advise the Secretary of State on matters relating to the supply of teachers.

The Scottish General Teaching Council

The functions listed above are basically those performed by the Scottish GTC today. Every four years teachers in Scotland directly elect to the Council eleven of their number from primary schools, a similar number from secondary schools and eight from colleges of education and further education; at the same time the universities, local government, the directors of education and the churches appoint their representatives to make the numbers up to forty-nine. The Council then appoints its members to a number of subsidiary committees which deal with its various statutory duties. These committees include the Admissions Committee, which admits new practitioners to the Register or, after carefully scrutinising their qualifications, experienced teachers from outside Scotland; and an Investigating and a Disciplinary Committee, which deal with complaints laid against teachers and have much the same powers as similar General Medical Council committees. Other committees give advice to institutions on the pedagogical contents of courses of teacher training (remember that the Council possesses the ultimate sanction of refusing to admit a teacher to its Register if it is not satisfied with his qualifications) and also advice to the Government on the supply of teachers. The Probation Committee requires a two-year probationary period for teachers; before the Council was established HM Inspectors had the responsibility of deciding whether a young teacher had successfully completed probation. Now, however, the Council requires the head teacher to submit a report at the end of the first year and again at the end of the second. The latter report must recommend to the Council to grant full registration, to extend probation for a further space of time or to withdraw registration altogether (probationers are entered provisionally on the Register when they begin to teach). Thus the competence of a person wishing to enter teaching is judged by his senior professional colleagues. Each year teachers in Scotland pay a small sum for re-registration; the Council is therefore self-financing and it seems to get through an enormous amount of work with fairly modest premises and a small staff. Critics of the Scottish Council expected rather too much of it too quickly. Some of its advocates hoped that, overnight, a General Teaching Council would revolutionise their profession, rid it of its incompetents and generally raise its standards to previously unattainable heights, and they have been disappointed. In fact, the task of a General Teaching Council must be a long-term one: gradually to require a higher level of qualifications for entry, to insist on more rigorous supervision of a teacher's apprenticeship years and to develop structures that will enable the inefficient to be eased out.

The Inadequate Teacher
No one would quarrel with the fair and effective way in which the Department of Education and Science from time to time rids us of a few undesirables and places their names on 'List 99', forbidding them to teach. The Department, however, has no power with which to get to grips with the small but obvious minority of hopelessly inept teachers who cause enormous problems for their schools, and who ought to be helped (or if necessary required) to find careers outside teaching. I hope that, if a General Teaching Council is created for England and Wales, it would seize this nettle and take steps to deal with those whose inadequacies mar their profession.

The Weaver Committee
In 1970, the Weaver Committee, with terms of reference from the then Secretary of State for Education and Science, Edward Short (now Lord Glenamara), recommended that a General Teaching Council be established with the co-operation of the teachers' unions and associations. The Weaver Report advocated that a Register of teachers should be kept, that registration should be compulsory and that responsibility for probation, teacher discipline (List 99) and advice on training should be transferred to the new body. It did not recommend that the reins of teacher supply should be allowed to

leave the hands of the Secretary of State. It was obviously feared that an independent Council would set higher entry qualifications which would constrict the teacher supply at a time when there was a great shortage of teachers and when the possession of a few O levels almost guaranteed entry to a course of teaching training. The Edward Short initiative sadly failed but there could be no better testimony to the perceived effectiveness of a General Teaching Council than a Government Report which refused to let it take charge of teacher supply in case it set standards which were too high!

Teaching as a Profession
Teachers have spoken about their 'profession' for a very long time; but the main criterion which distinguishes a 'profession' from other occupations is that its practitioners themselves, in effect, choose who shall join them as colleagues. At the moment local and central government officials perform this task for teachers; I and many other teachers suspect that we could do a better job.

Appendix Four

Teacher Training

In the summer of 1983, under the heading *Criteria and Mechanisms for the Approval of Initial Teacher Training Courses*, ACSET submitted detailed proposals to the Secretary of State for Education and Science and the Secretary of State for Wales regarding the future of teacher training courses. The following extracts are likely in due course to prove of particular significance.

The Mechanism for Professional Approval
The committee concluded that 'consistency across the country and considerations of wider accountability point, in the absence of a General Teaching Council, to the establishment by the Secretaries of State of a single national advisory council for the accreditation of initial training courses'.

Criteria for the Selection of Students
Institutions admitting students 'should be able to demonstrate that their selection procedures take into account the intellectual and personal qualities of candidates, and as far as possible their professional potential. Such procedures should in all cases include a personal interview with each candidate being considered for admission. Institutions should publicise the characteristics and qualifications to be sought in applicants. It is desirable that experienced practising school teachers should be asked to participate in the selection process, and should be given sufficient training to allow them to make an effective contribution'.

With regard to the personal qualities of applicants, the committee urged training institutions to 'look in particular for a sense of responsibility and for a blend of awareness, sensitivity, enthusiasm and ease of communication essential for successful teaching'.

Criteria for the Professional Aspects of Training

The committee emphasised the need for an intending primary school teacher to devote a substantial amount of time 'to the study of language and mathematics and the understanding of their significance across the curriculum', and the need for an intending secondary school teacher to appreciate the contribution which his or her specialist subject might make 'to the moral, aesthetic, social and academic development of pupils, relationships between the subject and other subjects, and an appreciation of the contribution which the subject makes to the curriculum as a whole'.

With regard to practical experience, the committee had this to say:

> The initial training of all potential teachers must include adequate attention to the variety of possible teaching methods which may be used, and the variety of settings in which teachers are employed. Substantial practical experience in schools is essential, amounting to at least 12 weeks for students on postgraduate courses, and at least 15 weeks for those on undergraduate courses. Both intermittent and block practice should be provided and a variety of different types of school experience should be included, for example, observation, child study, experimental work with small groups and small group teaching, studies of school organisation, involvement in extra-curricular activities and relationships with parents and the community. Where possible, courses should include a programme of visits, both before and after full-time teaching practice. It is essential that students should experience responsibility for a full class for a significant period, and have some responsibility for the organisation and planning of the children's work.

The committee felt that every training course should include certain essential elements 'both through teaching in the institution and through the careful structuring of school experience and teaching practice'. All training course proposals should show how it was intended to cover ten essential points:

1   the diversity that constitutes the full range of pupils, in terms of ability, behaviour, social background, ethnic and cultural origins, and the flexibility of response which may be required to build on the positive attributes which each child brings to the classroom.

2   the different ways in which children develop and learn, with particular reference to the development of language ability and of the capacity to understand mathematical concepts.

3   the assessment of pupil performance, and the appropriate levels of performance to be expected from children of differing ages, abilities, aptitudes and background, with an understanding of some of the more common learning difficulties and the potential of gifted children, and of ways of relating the demands made on individual pupils to their full capabilities.

4   methods of identifying children in ordinary schools with special educational needs, and knowledge of the specialist help available.

5   the potential contribution of new technologies to children's learning.

6   the variety of possible approaches to classroom management and control.

7   the processes of interaction and communication within groups and within a school and in particular an understanding of how the exchange of language between teacher and pupil influences the quality of learning.

8   the importance of staff collaboration and an appreciation of the contribution made by colleagues to the life of a school.

9   the need to appreciate the ways in which society and schools are interrelated, the important contribution which parents make to their children's educational development, and the relationship between the school curriculum and the adult world.

10 the need to provide opportunities for intending teachers to reflect on their classroom experience, to recognise and understand the processes which they have encountered at work, and to place them within the broader context of educational purposes.

The committee also gave some attention to the question of partnership between schools and training institutions. Practising teachers and local authority advisers should be involved in the 'planning, process and assessment of students' school experience and teaching practice, and should be fully prepared for this role'. The staff of institutions whose responsibility it is to teach pedagogy 'should have enjoyed success as teachers in primary or secondary schools, as appropriate, and should have continuing regular contact with classroom teaching'. Training institutions 'should establish or be associated with a teacher training committee on which local authorities, local schools and the institutions are represented and at which matters related to initial teacher training should be discussed on a regular and formal basis'.

Assessment of Students

On this important matter, the committee's recommendations to the Secretaries of State need to be quoted in full:

> Assessment of a student's performance as a potential teacher should not be confused with the assessment of academic performance. A separate judgement should be reached on his or her professional competence and practising schoolteachers should be involved in the assessment process. With regard to the specific matter of assessing teaching practice, schedules of assessment should cover the full range of activities and corresponding skills, and should be developed and applied in collaboration with staff in schools.

> Students should not be awarded a degree or certificate which carries qualified teacher status unless they have shown themselves to be competent in practical teaching. BEd and comparable undergraduate courses should be so planned that students' suitability for teaching is appraised as early as possible in their course, and those clearly unsuitable excluded from the course. If the academic work of these students is satisfactory, institutions should make every effort to offer them the opportunity of completing undergraduate study in a programme which does not lead to qualified teacher status, either in the same

institution or by transfer to another. Occasionally a student will reach the end of a 3 or 4 year course and show academic but not professional competence: in our view, such a student should be awarded an academic qualification which does not carry with it qualified teacher status. In no case should a qualification which carries qualified teacher status be awarded unless the student has achieved an appropriate level of professional competence.

Index